STANDARD GRADE

Drama

course notes

Elinor Kirk ✕ Robin Dewar

The authors would like to thank:
Anna Baughan
Alison Johnston
Lindsey Crickmay
Susanna Kirk
Hannah Donaldson

02/120508

ISBN 978-1-84372-488-9

Published by
Leckie & Leckie Ltd, 3rd Floor, 4 Queen Street, Edinburgh EH2 1JE
Phone: 0131 220 6831   Fax: 0131 225 9987
enquiries@leckieandleckie.co.uk   www.leckieandleckie.co.uk

Special thanks to
Anne Keay (manuscript review)
Project One Publishing Solutions, Edinburgh (Project management and editing)
The Partnership Publishing Solutions (Design and page layout)
Vicki Gausden (Illustrations)

A CIP Catalogue record for this book is available from the British Library.

® Leckie & Leckie is a registered trademark.
Leckie & Leckie is a division of Huveaux PLC

Acknowledgements
Leckie & Leckie has made every effort to trace all copyright holders.
If any have been inadvertently overlooked, we will be pleased to make the necessary arrangements.
We would like to thank the following for permission to reproduce their material:
Excerpts from *Gagarin's Way* and *Black Watch* by Gregory Burke reprinted with permission of Faber and Faber Ltd
Excerpt from *Passing Places* by Stephen Greenhorn copyright © 1998 reprinted with permission of the publishers: www.nickhernbooks.co.uk

CONTENTS

What Standard Grade Drama can do for you...

I was fortunate enough to go to a High School which offered Drama as a subject and I was able to study from a basic introduction, to Standard Grade, Higher and Advanced Higher. At school I was introduced to Scottish Youth Theatre who I worked with for many years. After school I spent a year working abroad before going to Dundee College to do their HNC in Performing Arts. I found this an excellent stepping stone – one which I believe helped me immensely in being accepted into the Royal Scottish Academy of Music and Drama. I graduated from the RSAMD in summer 2007 with a BA in Acting. During my second year at the Academy I took a term out to study in the USA at the California Institute of the Arts – this was a brilliant experience for me personally as well as educationally.

Since graduating from the RSAMD I've been lucky enough to work with some wonderful people in various areas of work. My work so far has ranged from radio plays with Radio 4 to film and TV with STV, BBC and Channel 4. My first professional stage job was playing Antigone at the Tron theatre in Glasgow and most recently I have joined the Dundee Rep Ensemble as part of their graduate scheme.

Many actors come into the profession having various levels of experience and each individual will find what's right for them. I found my studies at school an excellent start to my career, and Standard Grade Drama was particularly important. The course offers a wonderful combination of all aspects of the theatre. I was given the opportunity to explore work as a director, designer, writer, actor and so much more. It gave me the chance to taste a little bit of everything before deciding what was right for me.

I think that the benefits of studying Standard Grade Drama go much further that an introduction to the subject itself. The skills learnt and encouraged within the subject are undoubtedly precious tools which are of benefit in all walks of life. It certainly helped build up my confidence, self-esteem and people skills. I began to feel able to openly discuss my opinions in other classes and out of school in a work environment. I think that, more so than other subjects, drama has also helped me become better equipped to work in a team as well as on my own. And more than all of that, it's so much fun! I would wholeheartedly encourage anybody to choose Drama as a Standard Grade subject – the benefits are endless!

Hannah Donaldson

INTRODUCTION

It is very exciting to be revising this coursework book for Standard Grade Drama, now in its third edition. Since the first edition back in 1996, drama and theatre in Scotland have gone through a tremendous time of growth and innovation – new Scottish plays, new Scottish writers, Scottish actors in Hollywood and at last, a National Theatre for Scotland! Since Elinor wrote the original book we have both had wide practical experience of creating and presenting drama with different groups of actors as well as working with pupils in schools in various parts of Scotland.

There will be examples in the book of some of the new work which is going on – ideas to inspire you in your own drama learning.

More and more schools now offer Drama to pupils from S1 to S6. Many who were among the first to study Standard Grade and Higher Drama have gone on to further theatre training, and now have successful careers as actors, drama teachers, directors, lighting and sound technicians, stage managers and designers. Others have found the confidence and social skills gained from their drama studies have helped them pursue careers in areas such as the media, teaching, law and industry, while the creative freedom to develop ideas and put them into practice has enhanced the lives of many former drama pupils.

Now part of a well-established curriculum, Standard Grade Drama is a two-year course of study. Each school plans its own course to suit the needs of pupils.

A series of units which focus on specific skills, themes or relationships provides a structured sequence of drama activities. There have been some changes to the way the subject is taught and assessed and this book has been designed to include all of these.

There are different papers for each level – **Foundation**, **General** and **Credit**. You will sit either the Foundation plus General papers, or the General plus Credit papers. You may sit a practice exam which will let you know which papers you should be sitting, and your teacher will help you decide which papers to sit.

The Credit paper is more demanding and aimed at pupils who may want to go on to study Drama at Higher and Advanced Higher levels.

The course is broken down into three assessable elements or parts:

- **Creating**
- **Presenting**
- **Knowledge and Understanding**.

The **Creating** and **Presenting** elements are assessed in class. Your teacher marks your work in **Creating** and **Presenting**. You may achieve different grades at different times for each element:

Foundation	Grade 5 or 6
General	Grade 3 or 4
Credit	Grade 1 or 2

Towards the end of the course, your teacher will decide on a final grade for your **Creating** and **Presenting** work.

Knowledge and Understanding is assessed in a written examination at the end of your course. An external examiner marks your **Knowledge and Understanding** exam paper. The grade which appears on your certificate is based your performance in all three areas of the course, with equal marks awarded, one third of the total, for each element.

Using this book

This book suggests ways of giving your best performance in the three different elements of the course. You can use it from the beginning of your course right through to the final examination. It will help you with practical and written work.

You can't learn drama on your own from a book. The work you do in class, with your teacher and with others is what really matters. These course notes are for you to use:

- to add to what you are learning in class
- to give you the right words to use
- to provide an easy reference guide to assessment
- to give you examples of the kind of work done in **Creating** and **Presenting**
- to give you new ideas to try
- to give you advice on writing evaluations (part of **Presenting**)
- to help you prepare for the **Knowledge and Understanding** exam.

The book is divided into the same three sections as the course, with each section covering one of the three elements:

- **Creating**
- **Presenting**
- **Knowledge and Understanding**.

But they are all linked. The **Creating** section provides a guide to working from a stimulus. The **Presenting** section helps you shape your ideas into a presentation, using theatre skills. It also gives you guidelines for evaluating your own drama performances as well as presentations where you have been in the audience. You will find links in **Creating** and **Presenting** to detailed information in **Knowledge and Understanding**. What you write in the **Knowledge and Understanding** exam will test your knowledge of drama and theatre.

The **Knowledge and Understanding** section includes what you need to know about:

- Form and structure
- Staging
- Building a character
- Voice
- Movement
- Theatre arts
- Working from a script

Illustrations and examples from theatre practice are included all through the book.

Because it is important to know the right words for what you do in drama, there is a vocabulary list at the end of the book with words which relate to drama and theatre and what they mean. These are also the words you will be expected to understand and use in the written exam. These words are highlighted in **blue** when they first appear in the book. If you learn and use these in discussion and writing, you will put your ideas across clearly.

The book includes and range of **Hints** and **Activities**. Hints are practical suggestions to help you think about what you are doing. Some of the hints will help with your exams.

Activities are practical ideas for things you can do to help develop your skills and understanding. Some of them are things you can do on your own, and some are group activities.

In the **Knowledge and Understanding** section, each chapter closes with a **Learning more from being in an audience** section. These sections suggest some things to think about when you are watching a presentation and which can help with your own presentations.

But, above all, remember that drama is a creative, practical subject which allows you to express your own feelings and ideas. The process you go through in making a piece of theatre is as important as the end product. The skills you learn through listening, negotiating and making relationships as part of a team are more important than exam technique. And these are skills for life!

Hint

ACTIVITY

Learning more from being in an audience

THE DRAMA PROCESS – CREATING AND PRESENTING

The process of **creating** and **presenting** a piece of **drama** involves a number of different elements, and you need to learn how to fit all the different parts together. The process usually starts with a **stimulus**, and works through to a **presentation**, and will involve:

- responding to a stimulus
- offering ideas
- discussing and selecting ideas for situations and roles
- agreeing form, structure and conventions
- setting up space
- rehearsing
- reviewing
- adding theatre arts
- presenting to an audience
- evaluating.

CHAPTER 1
CREATING

In this chapter, you will learn about:

● investigating
● developing content and roles
● experimenting
● problem-solving

This section will help you to come up with ideas for drama, working with other people and getting the most out of discussion and **role-play**. Mostly you will be improvising, where you make up your own dramas.

Spontaneous improvisation is an instant **reaction** without preparation or discussion.

Rehearsed improvisation gives you time to think about how to **respond** to a stimulus. That's what we'll be looking at in this section.

Working from a stimulus

> *All drama is a response to a stimulus.*

What is a stimulus?

A **stimulus** is a **starting point** for drama, and can be anything which suggests ideas that can be **developed** into a **presentation**. Drama is a way of showing feelings and ideas. Like art and music, it allows us to share how we look at the world with others. To begin to create a drama, you need ideas. These can come from anything and anywhere. Drama is all around us – if you can see that, you will notice lots of things in everyday life which could be a starting point for drama.

For example, a stimulus could be an overheard conversation, a bunch of keys, a text message, a train ticket …

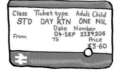

Examples of stimuli include:

- photographs
- a script
- a proverb or saying
- a costume

- objects or props
- music
- a sound effect
- words

- an old ballad
- song lyrics
- a map

A photograph

Who are the people in the picture?

Where are they?

What is going on?

What has happened just before this?

What will happen next?

An object or prop

Here are some things you could start with:

a single trainer   **a half-empty bottle of water**   **a sealed envelope**

These could all have stories behind them and dramas created from them.

An old ballad

(A ballad is a poem which tells a story)

> Ballad of the Sea Horse
>
> You landsmen and you seamen bold,
> Attention give to me
> While I a tragedy unfold
> Upon the briny sea.

Who is telling this story? What was the tragedy, the terrible thing that happened at sea? This could give you ideas for a drama about a shipwreck or some other danger. Maybe the storyteller was the only one who lived to tell the tale.

A script

A	What sort of creature?
B	It looks like....
A	Yes?
C	Yes?
B	A human child!
A	In the forest?
C	Impossible.
A	How did it get there?
C	You're dreaming.
A	Seeing things.
C	A child could not live in the forest.
B	I said it looks like a child, but it runs...like...a wolf!
A	No.

What could this be about? Who are A, B and C? What has B seen? What might happen next? Who or what has been seen in the forest?

Music

Here are three contrasting pieces you could **experiment** with:

The Harley Ashtray – Capercaillie; lively and fast
Mozart's *Flute and Harp Concerto*; slow, tuneful
In A Landscape – William Orbit; electronic, atmospheric

You might begin with everyone responding to the music – improvising movements such as running, stretching, turning, shivering, crawling, connecting, turning away.

These can developed into a **movement** piece or **dance drama**. The music could also be used to introduce a drama using words and **action**, or as background music.

A story or headline from a newspaper

PRISONER WINS LEGAL ACCESS
TO DAUGHTERS

Despite strong opposition from his ex-wife, a prisoner yesterday won access to the two children of his former marriage – which means they will be taken to see him in prison.

There are different ways of using this news story.

The prison visit could be acted out. You could find out the feelings of the different family members before or after it. One of the children might be trying to persuade her mother to let her see her father.

The mother could be discussing the case with her lawyer.

You might wonder what the father did to be put in prison – this could be shown.

Song lyrics

Song lyrics can suggest feelings – lost love, happiness, regrets...

> I was once like you are now,
> And I know that it's not easy
> To be calm, when you've found
> Something going on.
> But take your time, think a lot,
> Why, think of everything you've got,
> For you will still be here tomorrow, But
> your dreams may not.

This could be a drama about how a father and son get on at a particular time in their lives – the father is middle-aged, the son a teenager.

It could look at a family over a number of years, showing how relationships change. There are lines in this song which could be spoken in the drama and added to.

A proverb or saying

Proverbs or common sayings which everyone knows can be fun to work with.

You can create a story which shows what the saying means.

For example:

> When the cat's away the mice will play.

One idea would be for the cat (the parent in a family) to go away for the night, leaving the mice (the teenage son and daughter) to play. They have a party which could end up with the house being wrecked. This would work best as a drama if you showed how the people in it dealt with the problems.

Or you could show what happens when the cat (the boss) leaves the mice (the workers) in charge of an office or workshop. The workers have an important job to do. Things go wrong.

ACTIVITY

Here are two other proverbs you could use as starting points:

EVERY CLOUD HAS A SILVER LINING.

A STITCH IN TIME SAVES NINE.

A sound effect

The sound of wind in the trees and bird song could suggest a place for your drama – a park, or perhaps a forest.

Traffic sounds, footsteps and voices could suggest a city street.

Crashing waves, the sound of pebbles dragged by water might give you ideas for a drama at sea or on a beach.

A map

A map could suggest a mystery, or a secret meeting. Who drew this? Why? Who would see this? Could someone find this by accident? What might happen?

Hint

You will be used to working from starting points like these in your classwork. For the exam, you will be given a range of stimuli to work from in the Stimulus Paper. Being open to lots of ideas and trying them out all through your course will help you work quickly and creatively.

A costume

A blood-stained apron

A feathered hat

A pair of high-heeled boots

What **character** might be suggested by one of these? Could you develop a drama which tells their story?

Words

Words can describe strong emotions:

LOVE   HATE   BETRAYAL   DESPAIR

Any of these words could give you ideas for a powerful drama about relationships

Working in a group

Sharing ideas with others

When you are working from a stimulus, you will be sharing ideas and trying these out in a **group** with others.

Hint

It is really important to be able to work with other people.

In the Drama class, you don't need to be in a group with your friends. Sometimes it is better to work with someone you don't know so well. Your teacher needs to see you working with **different** people. Everyone should be able to work with everyone else.

Sometimes there is someone that no-one wants to work with. What if it's you? No-one likes to feel left out or not wanted. In Drama everyone has something to give to the group. But some people need extra help. To say 'We're not working with her,' or 'He never **contributes** anything' is hurtful and often unfair. Drama can help people get on with others, if they're given a chance.

Of course, if someone is behaving badly – shouting, refusing to listen, upsetting other people – you can't get on. That's when you'll need help from your teacher. But as you get better at working with others, your drama work will improve.

Often you have to work to a **deadline** (a time by which the task must be finished), so it is important not to waste time. There are some basic skills you can practise to make sure you and your group do good work in a short time:

- find a **space** to work in
- offer ideas
- listen to others
- say what you think – carefully!
- develop ideas
- try out ideas
- **select** and **reject** ideas
- solve problems and make notes
- role-play
- improvise

Find a space to work in

Make sure that everyone in the group can be seen and heard. Try not to be too close to another group – you don't want to be put off by hearing what they are saying. Start by making sure that everyone is clear about what to do. Have you all read or looked at the stimulus material? What has the teacher asked you to do? How long do you have to work on this? Setting yourselves a **time limit** for talking is useful. Sometimes it helps if someone notes down ideas, perhaps on a large sheet of paper with a marker pen. Then you have a record of what is said. You might each want to use this later to write your own notes.

Offer ideas

Everyone's ideas are useful and important, so always feel you can suggest something even if it doesn't seem very exciting or original. One way of getting lots of ideas is called **brainstorming**, when everyone gives their ideas and all the ideas are listened to or noted down. This can be a good way to begin.

Listen to others

Encourage quieter people to speak – help them by agreeing: 'That's worth thinking about,' and by asking questions: 'What would she do then?'

This can lead you on to another **scene**, perhaps just before the meeting, where you see what has happened to this person. Maybe a **prop** (an object to use in the drama) is needed:

> 'Let's give her a bag; it's got something in it that he wants.'

> 'He's not nearly frightening enough; he should be shouting at her.'

> **Hint**
>
> This is a time to try things out, not to criticise the way someone acts out ideas.

You could ask someone who has a suggestion to take over a role:

> 'Jack, you do the bad guy this time; show us how you think it should be done.'

But, remember, you are just being asked to adopt a role – to show you feel frightened or angry – not to develop a character in any depth. **There is no need to practise scenes at this point**. Decide if the idea works: if it does, note it for working on later; if not, try something else.

Using space and other resources

Space is wherever you are working. It's useful to decide where your acting area begins and ends.

Resources are anything available which you can make use of in your work.

Talk about what you might need

Don't start making detailed plans about how to use **scenery** or costumes at the moment. Experiment with any resources which are handy, for example:

- **rostra** (blocks or platforms)
- percussion instruments (drums, tambourines, bells)
- pieces of cloth

Make imaginary use of space and objects

> 'This area is the path – we could have a tree here for him to hide behind...'

'Then she takes out her mobile phone...'

'He suddenly sees the knife on the ground...'

Be ready to try ideas out in different ways

Here are some different ways you can experiment with ideas:

- speaking and action
- movement
- **frozen pictures**

> **Hint**
>
> You will find more ideas in **Forms** and **Conventions** in the *Knowledge and Understanding* section (page 33).

Try not to get carried away – one group acting out a noisy argument at full volume can make it hard for others to concentrate.

How is your work in Creating marked?

Your teacher will watch and listen to you as you are working and may use a checklist to note down what he or she sees you doing. Over your two-year course, he or she will build up a record of your abilities and progress in Creating.

This record will be used towards the end of the course to help the teacher decide on your final Creating grade. It is likely that you will make steady progress over two years, building up your skills as you gain experience.

> **Hint**
>
> By the end of the Creating process, your teacher should have seen you:
>
> - giving ideas
> - taking on different roles
> - using space and other resources (real or imaginary).

You and your group now have some ideas which you can develop for presenting to an audience.

CHAPTER 2
PRESENTING

In this chapter, you will learn how to **review** material you have developed in your Creating work through:

- making decisions
- rehearsing
- presenting your drama to an audience
- writing about how well you did all of this (evaluation)

You will find ideas to help you prepare your drama to show to an audience and advice on how to do your evaluations.

How are you going to present your drama?

Having studied the Creating section, you are now ready to move onto the next stage – preparing your work for presenting to an **audience**. From the Creating work you have done you have some ideas based on role-play and **improvised drama**, along with research – which can be developed into a presentation.

Content and form

You must first decide what your drama is about. This is called its **content**.

Then you must work out how to perform it so that an audience will understand it. This means deciding on the right form and structure.

Form is about the way the drama is presented – as a **play**, a dance drama or **mime**, and so on. Look at page 33 for a full list of the types of form you can use.

Structure

Structure is the way in which **time**, place and action are put together, for example:

- Scene 1 – morning, kitchen
- Scene 2 – afternoon, the park
- Scene 3 – evening, kitchen

A scene is a part of a drama which happens in one place and at one time. You'll read more about structure on pages 32 – 36.

Writing a scenario

It's useful to begin with a **scenario** (an **outline** of the drama) in which the **storyline**, or **plot**, is worked out. This should include details of the time and place of the action.

Imagine your group has chosen the word **Betrayal** as a stimulus.

Through discussion and role-play you have begun to create a drama which shows how a teenage boy betrays his younger sister's trust. You are now ready to develop this into a presentation with three scenes.

Kirsty Macfadyen 15   Carol Macfadyen 35 (their mother)

Alan Macfadyen 17 (her brother)   Craig Black 17 (Kirsty's secret boyfriend)

SCENE 1 (beginning)
Time: Saturday afternoon
Place: Kirsty's bedroom
Action
Kirsty is sitting on the bed, writing in her diary. Music playing on CD player. Alan comes in and questions her about rumours he's heard about her and Craig seeing each other. He turns down the music. He warns her that Craig has a bad reputation. Kirsty is angry and says it's none of his business. She says she's not stupid and makes him promise not to tell their mother about Craig. Alan promises reluctantly and leaves the room. Kirsty's phone beeps, she reads the screen, packs a bag with clothes and make-up and exits. A few moments later, Alan comes in and searches around the room. He finds the diary under the pillow on the bed. He reads it and his expression changes. He puts the diary in his pocket and leaves the room.

SCENE 2 (middle)
Time: Saturday evening
Place: the garden
Action
Carol is kneeling on the ground, weeding. Alan enters. Carol asks him if he's going out. He says no, he has studying to do. Alan asks where Kirsty is. Carol says she has gone to her friend Sarah's for a sleepover. Alan asks if she is sure about that and she asks why. Alan hints that she has friends Carol doesn't know about. Carol gets up, worried now and insists that he tells her more. Alan begins to tell her about Craig but she won't believe it. He pulls out the diary and hands it to her. As she reads we hear the diary entry in which Kirsty describes her plans to spend the night with Craig as a voice-over in Kirsty's voice. She asks Alan if she knows where Kirsty will be meeting Craig. Alan names a local pub. Carol puts the diary in her pocket and they both move quickly off stage.

SCENE 3 (end)
Time: Saturday night
Place: street outside pub
Action
Enter Carol and Alan. Carol checks that this is the right place. Alan begs her not to go in and make a scene. He says he will go in and speak to Kirsty. Carol pushes him aside and goes inside. Alan paces up and down, takes out his phone and presses some keys. Carol appears dragging Kirsty by the arm. Kirsty is crying and angrily denies that anything is going on with her and Craig. Carol starts shouting at her. Craig appears from inside the pub — Alan rushes at him. They fight and Alan punches Craig on the mouth. Kirsty goes to him. Carol pulls the diary out of her pocket and says she has the evidence to prove what is going on. Kirsty then turns on Alan saying he has betrayed her and she will never trust him again.

Before you start rehearsing (practising and improving your drama) you need to agree on how to use the space to stage your drama.

Where will your audience sit?

- In rows in front of the performing area?
- On three sides?
- How close do you want them to be to the **actors**?

What you decide depends on what you want them to see.

> **Hint**
>
> You can find more about **staging** your presentation on pages 37 – 39.

For the **Betrayal** drama, you might want your audience on three sides. That way they can be involved with what the family are feeling. They will be able to see the expressions on the performers' faces if they sit fairly close to the acting area.

Drawing a ground plan

A **ground plan** will give you enough information to set up your acting space for rehearsals and presentation.

A ground plan is a bird's eye view of the set, showing:

- the **acting area** – show where this begins and ends
- where the **audience** will be – write *audience* in the right place
- **exits** and **entrances** – where performers come in and go out – can be shown by a *door symbol* where a door flat would be used or by *arrows* when walls and doors are imaginary or do not exist
- **furniture** or **rostra** (see **key** on page 88 for symbols)

The **set** must be **viable**, meaning that it will actually work. The set must also **leave space** for the actors to move around the acting area.

The audience **must** be able to see the action and the actors.

Your plan should be a bird's eye view of the acting area, drawn roughly to scale meaning that furniture should be the right size for the acting space.

It **must** have a key to show what symbols you have used.

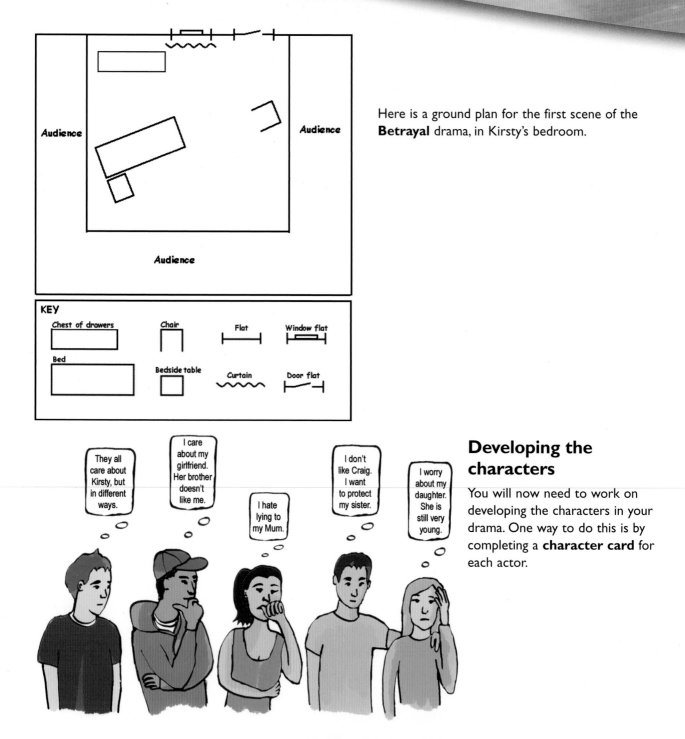

Here is a ground plan for the first scene of the **Betrayal** drama, in Kirsty's bedroom.

Developing the characters

You will now need to work on developing the characters in your drama. One way to do this is by completing a **character card** for each actor.

Here is a very simple one for Kirsty:

Full Name: Kirsty Macfadyen	*Age:* 15

Occupation: School pupil and part-time shop assistant

Physical description: Young looking for 15, shoulder length naturally brown hair, open, pleasant expression

Personality: Quiet, rather shy. Fond of children and animals. Close to her mother and brother, especially since her father left when she was 10.

You can also add more detailed information on costume, **make-up**, **voice**, movement, behaviour and **status**. **Relationships** with other characters are also very important and should be carefully worked out. In this case, the relationship between Kirsty and Craig is central.

Kirsty is having a serious relationship with Craig Black, a 17 year old who has left school and has a job as a mechanic. She looks up to him and hopes they will have a future together. She will not believe any of the rumours about him taking drugs and being violent. She knows he has done some bad things in the past but believes him when he says he has changed. She has fallen out with some of her friends over Craig. She has kept their relationship secret although she hates lying to her mother but knows that her mother will not agree to her seeing Craig.

> **Hint**
>
> You can find more about building a character pages 40 – 44.

Theatre arts

Theatre arts include **set**, **make-up**, **costume**, **sound**, **lighting** and **props**.

They can make your drama better, more interesting and believable. Using them can be very creative and enjoyable and gives you the chance to practise your skills in theatre **technology**.

Time is often short and resources have to be shared among groups – this can be frustrating. So, you have to plan and negotiate with others and your teacher.

This means talking about difficulties and sorting them out fairly. If you have to share space with other groups, you will have to think about the time and effort it takes to **strike the set**, or clear it of scenery, furniture and props.

Start by discussing as a group **what you need to do** and **how you can get it done**. **Be realistic** about what you can do in the time you have and with the resources available.

I've done some make-up designs at home.

I've brought in this hat for Craig to wear.

I found this diary for Kirsty.

How about this mobile for the brother?

Can we get our lighting ideas sorted out?

Here are some ideas for using theatre arts in the **Betrayal** drama:

Scene 1	
Set	bed, chair, bedside table
Set dressing	duvet, pillow, cushions, furry toys, posters, clothes, shoes
Props	CD player, diary, pen, mobile phone, handbag, make-up, short skirt, high-heeled shoes, earrings, necklace
Costume	**Kirsty:** jeans and t-shirt, socks **Alan:** jeans, sweatshirt, trainers
Make-up	None
Lighting	Sun filtering through window curtain
Sound	Music in background, mobile phone beep
Scene 2	
Set	large plants in pots
Props	tray of plants, small gardening fork, basket with weeds in it, diary,
Costume	**Carol:** old jeans and man's shirt, sandals **Alan:** as scene 1
Make-up	**Carol:** pale foundation, dark eye make-up, shadows under eyes to create a tired look
Lighting	Summer evening sunshine into twilight
Sound	Birdsong
Scene 3	
Set	Street with flats forming front of building with opening door flat to represent pub, rubbish (cans, crisp packets, newspaper on floor), lamp-post
Props	mobile phone, diary
Costume	**Carol:** as scene 2 but wet **Alan:** as scene 1 but wet **Kirsty:** short skirt, low cut top, high heeled shoes, jewellery **Craig:** jeans, leather jacket over slogan t-shirt
Make-up	**Carol:** as before **Kirsty:** heavy make-up, exaggerated eyes and lips **Craig:** blood capsule in mouth for fight
Lighting	Dark, street lights, bright lights when pub door opens
Sound	Rain, sounds of laughter, glasses, music from pub.

Some questions you might be asked

There are a few questions you might be asked about your work:

- what is the **purpose** of your drama?
- who is your **target audience**?
- which aspect of your drama might have most **impact** on your audience and why?
- how could theatre arts **enhance** your drama?

What is the purpose of your drama?

In the **Betrayal** drama, the purpose is to **explore family relationships**, between brother and sister, mother and son, mother and daughter and show the impact of a betrayal of trust. It raises questions about confidentiality – when is it right to break a promise?

Who is your target audience?

The target audience could be:

- your own class?
- primary school children?
- adults?

Is your drama suitable for your audience? You might decide that the **Betrayal** drama would appeal most to teenagers. You can find more about target audience in pages 32 – 33.

Which aspect of your drama might have the most impact on your audience and why?

The fight scene in the street is the explosion of the **tension** which has been building up. The realisation by Kirsty that her brother has injured her boyfriend is the first shock for her, the second that he has betrayed her by letting their mother read her private diary.

How could theatre arts enhance this impact?

This could be done through use of **lighting** effects – darkness and shadows, with a sudden bright light from the pub door.

Sound – rain, shouts and noise from the pub – would add to the **atmosphere** of discomfort.

Kirsty's heavy **make-up** makes her look much older and more sophisticated – a shocking contrast to her innocent appearance in Scene 1. The **blood capsule** would provide an unpleasantly **realistic** trickle of blood from the corner of Craig's mouth. The diary is an important **prop** which could end up trampled on the ground at the end.

Some tips for working on your drama

Decide who is going to be in charge of each task

Make sure everyone knows **who is in charge** of tasks and that they know what to do and where to get help.

Plan ahead – someone may be absent at a critical point. Have someone else lined up to help out.

Troubleshooting

In school, several groups will probably be trying to do technical work at the same time. This can cause problems. You must sort out **who** does **what**, and **when**.

Be prepared to be **flexible** – get on with rehearsing while another group position their lights. Maybe someone could make a sound recording at home and save time in class. Try to make sure **everyone** in the group has a job to do – if two of you have a scene to **rehearse**, other group members could be doing make-up designs or writing up props lists.

Often, ideas are too complicated and ambitious for the time and resources available. Sometimes a really good idea will have to be changed because it just can't be done. Even if you can't use it, you can write later about what you **would** have done. Ideas are never wasted – they can be used another time. Stop now and then to review progress, discussing and noting down problems. Give your opinions about what is working and what is not. Suggest improvements. Being able to adapt and **simplify** can help your group meet deadlines.

Last minute technical problems **always happen**: be ready for this. Have scissors, tape, safety pins, torch, copies of plans and lists handy. A spare CD player or alternative spotlight can allow the show to go on.

For all technical work, keeping careful notes, plans and lists is absolutely essential. **Keep everything safely in a folder in school** and make sure everyone in the group knows where it is.

Sometimes you will want someone to be your **stage manager**, to be responsible for everything on the technical side while the rest of you are acting. This can be a very rewarding and challenging job. Doing this at some point in your Standard Grade course will help you understand more about using theatre arts.

The performance

The audience is waiting.

Your mouth goes dry and you've forgotten everything.

You take a few deep breaths and relax your shoulders.

The lights go up, and you're on!

Amazingly, you get through it, remembering what you did in rehearsals.

You even add something new and it works.

Someone makes a mistake but the rest of you help them out.

The audience doesn't notice.

You get to the end, much faster than you expected.

The audience claps.

They liked it!

You've done it!

And it feels great… But now you're going to have to **evaluate** it.

Hint

You can find more about theatre arts on pages 59 – 65.

Evaluating the drama

Evaluation is the process of:

- reflecting
- reviewing
- target-setting.

Continuous evaluation is what you do while you are creating and presenting, noticing how well you are doing as you go along

- Do this on your own, **reflecting by yourself** on how rehearsals are going and making notes.
- Do this through **talking with your group** about your work together.
- Give **opinions** on what is working and say why (**justify** your views).
- Do this through **listening** to your teacher's ideas and suggestions.
- Suggest **improvements**.

Summative evaluation is about judging your work after doing it, learning from experience and setting future targets

- Do this on your own, **reflecting on your own performance**. Write down some words that your presentation made you think of, such as: feelings, understanding, **conflict**, problems, trust, atmosphere, laughter, tension.
- Do this through **asking your own group** and your **audience** what they thought. Talk about the **best bits**, the **worst bits**, what you felt pleased about and what you would change if you did it again.
- **Watch your performance** by recording on video if possible
- Get **feedback** from your teacher
- Ask yourself if you **achieved** what you set out to do and what **targets** you would aim for in the future

When you are writing evaluations, say things like

- 'I suggested ...'
- 'I think ...',
- 'I was disappointed that ...',
- 'I was pleased when ...'

Evaluation of your own presentation

When you write about your own presentation, be **honest** about the way things worked or didn't work. Include these points in your evaluation:

- Say **what** you were asked to do and **how** you decided on what material to develop for your presentation. Be clear about your **personal contribution** right from the start.

- Mention ideas that you put forward, even if they were rejected. Write about how the **group worked out a storyline**, how you decided who should play which part.

- Were there **disagreements**? Say what the problems were and how you **solved** them. Give reasons for your decisions.

- What **opinions** did you offer? What worked well? What didn't? Why?

- What **improvements** did you suggest? Did they make a difference?

- Include what ideas you had about the **character** you were to play. Did you have any other tasks, for example, finding music or making props?

- Say how **rehearsals** went. Were there particular problems – use of space, entrances and exits, developing characters – that had to be sorted out?

- Describe how you went about **developing your own character**. Mention **language** and voice, movement, working on relationships through improvised drama and discussion. Did your character change?

- Say what use your group made of **theatre arts**. Give reasons for what you chose to use, any problems you came across and how these were solved.

- State what your **group's aim** was in the presentation. What did you want your audience to think and feel?

- Say what **made it work**. What did you **learn**?

- Remember to **justify** everything you say.

Talking and writing about what you have seen other people do

When you've seen a really good presentation, either in the classroom or in a theatre, you're left with a feeling of 'Wow! That was amazing!'

That's what you want to build on when you do an evaluation of others.

What made it special?

What was there that gave you that feeling – the 'tingle factor' – that has you sitting straight up in your seat?

Was it the actor who made you laugh till you cried?

Was it the set, where the **revolving stage** swung round to show the soldiers ready for battle?

Was it the eerie bell tolling on a darkened stage?

Work on this in the same way as your evaluation of your own presentation. Use your own knowledge and experience to help you judge others.

Before writing (or recording) your evaluation of others:

Write down some words that the presentation made you think of: powerful, exciting, laughter, effects, music, fighting, wonder, real, movement, colour, mood, startling.

Sit down and talk with someone else who saw it. Talk about the best bits, the worst bits, and what you remember most clearly.

Look at the **programme**. There is lots of useful information in this about the play, the actors, the director, the designer and others.

Talk with your teacher. He or she may have some ideas of his or her own, or some questions for you.

Include these points in your evaluations of other presentations

- Say **where** you saw it. Did you see the presentation in a big theatre or a school hall? How was it **staged**? Were you close to the actors? What made you feel **involved**?

- Say **briefly** what happened in the presentation.

- Who was it aimed at? (**target audience**?)

- Include the **best** moments. Why were they the best?

- Describe a couple of **good acting performances** in some detail (use your programme for names). You know enough about building a character to be critical.
- Discuss **theatre arts**. How did make-up, costume, sound and/or music, lighting, set and props help make the presentation special?
- Say what **made it work**. How did it make you **feel**? What did it make you **think** about?
- What was your overall **opinion**?
- How do you think it could have been **improved**?
- Remember to **justify** everything you say.

How is your work in Presenting marked?

For your practical work, your teacher will watch you and listen to you as you are working and may use a checklist to note down what he or she sees you doing. Over your two-year course, he or she will build up a record of your skills and progress in Presenting.

He or she will also be marking the evaluations you will be doing, which could be written or recorded. Towards the end of the course, your two best evaluations, one of self and one of others, will be chosen. Your teacher will give you a grade for these. This grade will be combined with your final grade for your practical work to give an overall grade for Presenting.

Hint

By the end of the Presenting process, your teacher should have seen you:

- contributing to planning
- **portraying** characters
- showing you can use Theatre Arts and technology
- evaluating your own drama work and the work of others.

You can now go on to the Knowledge and Understanding Section to study Drama in more detail to prepare for your exam.

KNOWLEDGE AND UNDERSTANDING

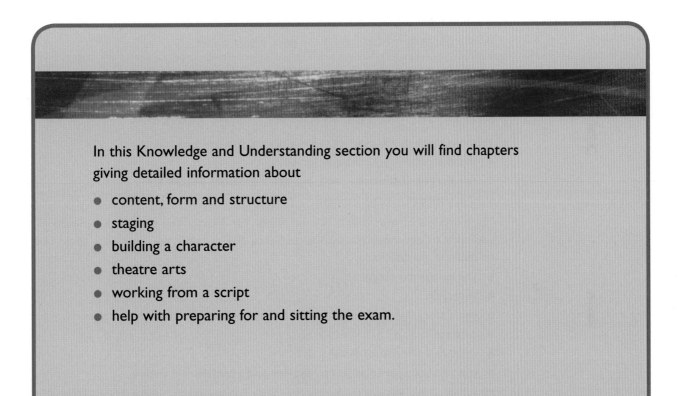

In this Knowledge and Understanding section you will find chapters
giving detailed information about

- content, form and structure
- staging
- building a character
- theatre arts
- working from a script
- help with preparing for and sitting the exam.

CHAPTER 3
FORM AND STRUCTURE

In this chapter, you'll learn about:

- the **purpose** – your reason for presenting a drama
- the **target audience** – who will get most from watching your presentation
- the **content** – what happens in your presentation.

Purpose, target audience and content

When you are developing ideas for a drama, you need to consider:

- the **purpose** – your reason for doing it
- the **target audience** – who will get most from watching
- the **content** – what happens.

The **purpose** of your drama is your reason for doing it. You start with something you want to **communicate** to an audience. For example, you may want to do one or more of the following:

- put across a message
- entertain
- tell a story
- educate
- explore a **theme** or **issue**
- use audience participation to explore and experience a theme.

Deciding on the **target audience** for your presentation is about deciding which group (or groups) of people will get most out of watching your performance.

You may have been thinking from the start of your work about who would be a suitable audience for your drama. By the time you are ready to present it, you will have a clearer idea. You might feel that your presentation is for a general audience – all ages, male and female, or that it would be appreciated more by a **specific** group of people.

Is it aimed at your own age group? **Topics** like bullying, divorce or drugs could be relevant to a teenage audience, especially if the main characters are young people. Perhaps your drama would appeal to a younger audience – a fantasy adventure or a puppet play. You might have chosen an issue which is relevant to all age groups – war or global warming.

How you put your ideas across will be influenced by your target audience. Using music from the current charts would appeal to a teenage audience; swearing would not be acceptable in a children's show.

The **content** of your presentation is what actually happens – the material you make use of and the subject matter of your drama.

Having decided what you want to communicate in your drama (its content), you now have to decide how to do this (its form and structure).

Form, conventions and structure

Form is the overall **style** of your presentation. A range of different styles are shown in the table below.

a **play** (scripted or improvised)	in which a story is acted out
dance drama	a way of presenting a drama using dance moves
melodrama	a sensational or exaggerated piece of drama
mime	a form of **stylised** movement which can create an illusion of reality
monologue	a drama with one character speaking
movement	a way of expressing ideas, emotions and relationships through using the body
musical	a drama where the story is told through songs and music
pantomime	theatrical entertainment with songs, **comedy** and audience participation usually based on a fairytale
comedy	a drama which makes the audience laugh and has a happy ending
tragedy	a drama about unhappy events with a sad ending
docu-drama	a documentary-style presentation, based on true events
Forum Theatre	*Augusto Boal*'s very specific form of theatre using audience participation to shape the outcome of the drama

Within the overall form you may use different dramatic **conventions**. These are alternative ways of presenting all or part(s) of your work, shown in the table.

dialogue	conversation involving two or more characters
flashback	a scene **set** in the past
flashforward	a scene set in the future
freeze frame	action frozen in time
frozen picture or **tableau**	a stage picture, held without movement
slow motion	movement performed at a slowed down speed
narration	where someone tells the story as it is acted out
voice-over	recorded speech played during a drama
aside	a remark to the audience only
soliloquy	one character, alone **on stage**, speaking their thoughts

Structure is the way in which your drama is put together in terms of time, place and action. You can choose a **linear** structure where the action unfolds from beginning to middle to end, or a **non-linear** structure where the action unfolds through shifts in time and/or place.

You need to decide on the **focus** of your drama. Key scenes, characters and events will help the audience understand your purpose. By highlighting important moments in a variety of ways you can make sure that your purpose is clear and your message communicated. (See pages 35 – 36 for more on mood, atmosphere and tension.)

You could start with a feeling which you want to explore. Drawing a diagram like the one below can give you ideas. This one is about **fear**:

Here is a **linear** (chronological) scenario which could be developed from the diagram:

THE MUGGING

Beginning

A teenager is walking home at night (time) along a lighted street (place) with two friends (action). They reach the park gates. He says goodbye to his friends.

Middle

He sets out to take a short cut through the park. He starts to feel frightened, looking around nervously, jumping at any sounds. He starts whistling to himself and walks faster as he hears footsteps behind him. A woman walking her dog catches up, says 'Good evening,' and walks on. He hears footsteps again. This time, two men come up behind him. One grabs hold of him, the other threatens him, asking for money. They take his wallet and kick him to the ground. They run off.

End

He lies there, hurt and frightened. The dog walker comes back, finds him and helps him to his feet.

Here is a **non-linear** structure using some of the same ideas, but with no clear indication of time and place:

> ### NIGHTMARE
>
> A girl lies curled up in the centre of the performing space. She has a pillow, a blanket and a doll.
>
> There is eerie music and four masked figures creep in at floor level. They take away her protective symbols – the pillow, doll and blanket – tossing them to one another, then off to the side.
>
> She is awake now and they pull her to her feet, then push her back and forward, chanting in turn; 'You're ugly', 'You're a failure', 'Nobody likes you', 'You're stupid'. She sinks down, covering her ears, making herself as small as possible as the voices get louder and the figures more menacing.
>
> The figures now have a large piece of red cloth which they hold at each corner. They make it billow up above her, then let it fall to cover her. She screams. The figures shrink to the floor and creep away, pulling the cloth with them. Two of them return her props and she lies down peacefully.

Mood, atmosphere and tension

Mood and **atmosphere** concern the feelings of the audience. When we watch a drama we respond to what we see and hear.

Tension is what keeps us interested and is the driving force of a drama. You can create tension through:

- movement
- shock or surprise
- silence
- action
- conflict and confrontation
- mystery
- relationships and status
- threat or pressure
- **dramatic irony** (where the audience knows something not all characters are aware of).

ACTIVITY

Look back at the two sample scenarios on Fear. Can you find some examples of techniques used to create and build tension?

As an actor you can create mood and atmosphere and heighten tension through:

- movement
- pace
- pause
- silence
- voice
- eye contact
- **moves**
- **physical** contact
- contrast
- **positioning**
- **timing**.

You can use **theatre arts** to create mood and atmosphere and heighten tension through:

- staging
- set
- lighting
- sound effects
- music
- costume
- props
- make-up
- **masks**
- **special effects**

Learning more from being in an audience

Whatever type of presentation you are watching, you should be aware of what the content is, and how it is being presented. What forms and conventions are being used? What is the structure of the presentation? How is tension built up? What are the key moments? What ideas could you use in your own work?

If you enjoyed a presentation, was this because it had things in it which appealed to you? If you were bored, was this because the play was aimed at an older audience, rather than because it was just not very good? Look at how other people in the audience react. Maybe they are laughing as they recognise characters and stories from their own lives. Is it important to be able to relate to what you see?

When you are affected by what you see, try to work out what it is that brings a lump to your throat, what makes you laugh, what makes you angry. What was the meaning behind what happened? What mood and atmosphere was created? What techniques were used to heighten tension?

At a pantomime or a children's show, the actors often get the audience to join in. What effect does this have? You can learn a lot about purpose, content, form, structure, mood, atmosphere and tension by seeing as many different types of presentations as you can: pantomimes, musicals, serious plays, comedies, opera, dance, children's shows, puppet shows, street theatre.

You will like some more than others, but you can learn from any live theatre experience. Don't underestimate the importance of presentations you see in school. It is helpful for Standard Grade pupils to have an audience; Higher students must have an audience for their presentations. Take any opportunities you can to see their work.

CHAPTER 4
STAGING

In this chapter you will learn about different types of staging and venues:

- end on presentation
- theatre in the round
- thrust presentation
- proscenium arch presentation
- avenue presentation
- promenade presentation

Staging your presentation

Once you have decided what your presentation is to be about and how you will perform it, you need to think about **how to present it** to an audience.

The acting area is the part of the available space used by the actors when acting. The acting area may be empty or occupied by the set (scenery and furniture) and there must be places where the actors can enter and exit the acting area easily. **Staging** is about the way the acting area is positioned relative to the audience. This involves working out where the audience will be as they watch the drama.

The audience will sit in the **auditorium**. In a theatre, there is usually fixed seating, with a raised stage, often at one end. In your drama studio or classroom, there will be a number of options. If you have rostra which can be used to build a platform, you can have a raised stage. You may have seating which can be raised. Raising the height of the audience or the acting area can make the drama easier to see. It's important to think about the **sight lines**, so that you can be sure that everyone in the audience can see all the action on stage.

The back 'wall' of the stage, which could be a fixed screen or suspended backdrop, is called the **cyclorama** and can be lit to create different effects.

There is usually an off-stage area where actors are out of sight of the audience. The off-stage area is often curtained off from the stage area using **blacks**. In a stage with a proscenium arch, this area is called the **wings**. There may also be an area on the stage in front of the curtain called the **apron**. Large theatres will have an area above the stage called the **flies** which allows actors and scenery to be flown onto the stage area on pulleys and wires.

Sometimes actors may simply sit on chairs or benches at the edge of the acting area when not performing. It is important to decide where your actors will go when they leave the stage.

Different types of staging

Depending on space and resources, here are some different types of staging to consider for your presentation:

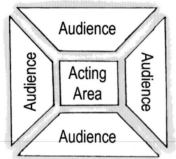

End on

The audience is seated at one end, and is **end on** to the acting area at the other end. This gives all the audience the same view of the action, with more space in the acting area which can be used for scenery. It does distance the audience more, however, from what is going on.

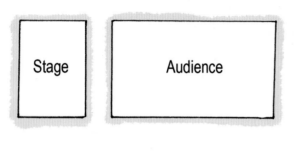

Theatre in the round

In **theatre in the round** staging, the audience is seated on all sides, with acting space in the centre. This allows the audience to see the drama from different viewpoints; they are close to the action; actor's entrances and exits can be from all four corners. There will be times when some of the audience have a restricted view; this would have to be considered in rehearsal.

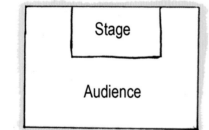

Thrust

Thrust staging has the audience seated on three sides. This has the advantages of theatre in the round, but with a 'back wall' which gives more room for a set and allows the audience a better view of the action.

Proscenium arch

The **proscenium arch** is the traditional 'picture-frame' stage, raised, with front curtains; the audience seated in front of the performing area

Avenue

In **avenue** staging, the audience is seated on two sides of the acting area. Fashion shows are often presented like

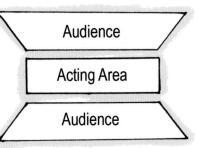

this, with a catwalk for the models. This can be good for a drama with lots of action, where actors pass through the performing space close to the audience.

Promenade

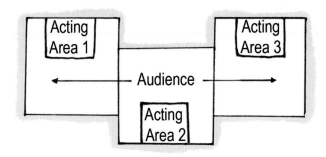

Promenade staging has the audience following the action on foot, moving from one location to another. This allows real audience involvement, especially in crowd scenes, but can be tiring for the spectators who will not always see everything.

Venue

A **venue** is any place where a drama is presented: a theatre, a classroom, a school hall are obvious places, but you could see a drama presentation in a park, a church, a street, a supermarket, a shopping mall, a car park… anywhere, in fact, that you could have space for performers and an audience. There is a theatre company in Scotland which presents drama in non-theatre spaces, even in people's living rooms! At the other end of the scale are the big theatres in our major cities. Most of these theatres have a proscenium arch, and the audience sits in the **stalls** (closest to the stage), in the **circle** (above the stalls) or in the **balcony** (above the circle). These theatres will also have a **green room** where the actors wait when they're not on stage.

Most venues will use curtains, or **tabs**, to separate the acting area from the audience.

Not all drama is suitable for every venue

A street performance would have to be eye-catching, easily understood and fairly short to capture the attention of passers-by. A church or a castle would be a good setting for a historical drama, with opportunities for using different levels. A school hall might need careful arrangement of seating to allow everyone to see, possibly using a **floorcloth** (a piece of heavy canvas) to define the acting area.

Learning more from being in an audience

Noticing how a presentation is staged can give you ideas for your own work. If you see the same play at two different venues, the atmosphere at each can be quite different. This can be because of the relationship between audience and actors. You might feel very involved, as if you are part of the action, in a small studio theatre with the audience on three sides. Watching a spectacular musical on a proscenium stage in a large theatre, you could feel swept along by what you see, but at more of a distance.

CHAPTER 5
BUILDING A CHARACTER

In this chapter you will learn the different elements you need to consider to create realistic characters. These elements include:

- age
- background
- personality
- interests
- name
- appearance
- language and voice
- movement, body language and gestures
- motivation.

Right, we need to get characters sorted. Who wants to be Kirsty?

I could be the Mum.

You be the boyfriend Colin. I'd like to be the brother.

Laura, how about you playing Kirsty? I'd really like a smaller part this time.

That'd be good. I'd like to be Craig. It'll be a laugh being the bad guy!

Getting into character

An essential part of any drama is convincing an audience that the characters are real people and that what happens in the drama is important and believable.

There are lots of elements to a character, and you may need to work on all of them to make the character convincing. You need to be careful not to fall into the trap of relying on **stereotypes**, which can give an exaggerated portrayal of a character.

Age

It is important to be clear about how **old** your character is. In your group, you have to decide how old each character is in relation to the others. This has to make sense. A woman of 30 is unlikely to have a son aged 20! A man born in 1935 could have childhood memories of the Second World War. Your character's age will help you decide on a believable history for that person.

Background

A real person has a history. Their **background** (what has happened to someone in their life before the events of the drama) makes them the person they are. **Experiences** in childhood, family life, at school, with friends, at work, successes and failures, problems with relationships – all of these affect the way someone is now.

Personality

Your **personality** is the way you are – you might be out-going or shy, cheerful or moody. A happy, optimistic person will cope better with a crisis than someone who already feels defeated by life. None of us are the same all the time, but other people will often describe us as being a certain kind of person. Thinking about your character's personality will help you work out how he or she might **behave** in different situations.

Interests

Having ideas about someone's **interests** and **hobbies** can help build your character. These will be linked with the other decisions you are making about the person. A shy, middle-aged man might be keen on bird-watching; an energetic teenage girl could be a karate enthusiast. If you know what your character does in their spare time, you can bring that into the drama.

Name

Don't use your own name. Some people use their own name in role, but it does tend to hold them back from developing their character as a separate **individual**. Giving your character a **separate identity** from yourself will help you make the part come alive for you and the audience.

Mum and Dad should really have names of their own – being parents is only one part of their identity.

Names should fit the age of your character. No-one over 30 is likely to be called Bailey or Chantelle; very few children are called Albert or Hilda today. Remember to give your character a surname as well as a first name.

In a movement piece, your characters may not have names, but they could be 'Masked Figure One', 'The Leader', or 'The Victim'.

Appearance

Some definite ideas about appearance will help you and the group to **picture this person**. What sort of clothes does he or she wear? Is he or she smart or scruffy; well-built or skinny? Be sensible about what each person can realistically achieve through make-up and costume. If you are small and lightly-built, playing a tall, broad-shouldered rugby player might not be a good idea! Boys playing female parts or girls playing male roles can sometimes be acceptable, but it is usually better to play someone of your own sex.

Language and voice

Getting the **voice right** can help you become your character easily in rehearsal and **performance** – it is worth working on (see pages 46 – 49).

Movement, body language and gestures

Movement, **body language** and gestures can tell the audience a great deal about a character (see pages 50 – 58).

Age and physical fitness can affect the way someone moves. An actor can play a young child by moving in a much quicker, less controlled way than an adult, or an old person by moving more slowly and stiffly.

Some people like to find the right shoes for their character – a farmer in Wellington boots will walk very differently from a secretary in smart shoes.

Develop **suitable actions** for your character as you rehearse. Some activities, such as combing your hair, unfolding and reading a newspaper, or chopping vegetables, give you something to do and help the audience believe in you.

ACTIVITY

Practise walking, standing, sitting down and getting up in role. Think about anything that might affect your character's movement – a tight skirt, a painful hip joint, carrying a heavy case. Giving your character a particular habit or mannerism can be useful – flicking hair back, nail-biting, standing with hands on hips, rocking backwards and forwards. First, however, you have to become aware of, and avoid, your own habits! Do you play with your hair, pull your sleeves down over your hands or always sit with your legs crossed?

Motivation

Motivation is the reason behind your character's **behaviour**. It is important in helping you understand how his or her mind works. Finding out about your character's motivation will help you know how to react, what to do and how to speak in different situations.

Ways of exploring and developing a character

There are lots of different ways of exploring and developing a character. Here are some to try out.

Hot-seating

One way to find out about a character's motivation is to spend some time in rehearsal **hot-seating** each character in turn. This can make a big difference to your **portrayal** of the character, because you have to think as that person, not as yourself.

ACTIVITY

Place one chair in a prominent position, facing the rest of the chairs in a semi-circle. Each actor sits on the 'hot seat' in role and the rest of the group ask questions about feelings, events, other characters, about hopes and fears, past and future. The actor has to answer in role but has the right not to answer questions which their character would not wish to respond to.

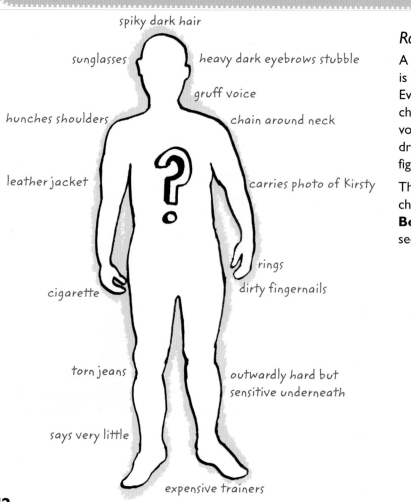

spiky dark hair

sunglasses   heavy dark eyebrows stubble

gruff voice

hunches shoulders   chain around neck

leather jacket   carries photo of Kirsty

rings

cigarette   dirty fingernails

torn jeans   outwardly hard but sensitive underneath

says very little

expensive trainers

Role on the wall

A large outline drawing of a figure is put on the wall or blackboard. Everyone offers ideas about this character's appearance, behaviour, voice, interests, habits etc. which are drawn on and written around the figure.

This example is based on the character of the boyfriend in the **Betrayal** drama from the Presenting section.

Thought-tracking

In **thought-tracking**, a character speaks their thoughts out loud. A good way of doing this is to create a group sculpture (like a tableau) showing a moment from the drama in which there are several different characters. On a given signal, each comes to life and speaks their thoughts about the situation they are in.

ACTIVITY

Create the ball scene from 'Cinderella' where the Prince and Cinderella are dancing, watched by the Ugly Sisters. Freeze it and find out what each character is thinking about the situation.

Thought-tunnel

In a **thought-tunnel**, two lines are formed to make a narrow 'passageway'. As a character walks through the space, each person in the line comments on their situation.

Voices in the head

Voices in the head are similar to thought-tunnel – here the character is recalling words said by others about him or the situation he is in. This could be done with the actor sitting or standing with others standing around him speaking in turn. (See the example of the **Nightmare** drama in the Structure section on page 35.)

Hint

Get into two equal lines opposite each other. One person takes on the role of a runaway teenager and walks through the 'tunnel'. As she passes each person, a comment is made, e.g. 'Maybe she's made a mistake,' 'Her mother is in a terrible state', 'Where will she sleep tonight?

Writing in role

Writing in role is another way of getting into the mind of your character.
This could be:

● a diary of the worst day in your life
● a letter to your mother in which you tell her how you feel
● your life story.

Relationships

Relationships with other people are at the **heart of drama**. Parents and children, friends and enemies, bosses and workers. Often people fight and argue – this **conflict** is what is interesting.

You need to know why your character behaves, for example, in a relaxed way with some people and is tense and awkward with others. Working in role with others in your group, putting your characters into different situations, can help you find out more.

Choose two adult characters and improvise a scene in which they are young children playing together.

Think about how characters respond to one another. For example, a child enters during a scene where his mum and dad are arguing. Where does he move to? Why? What does the mum do? What about the dad? This is **interaction** (how characters react and respond to each other).

Status

Status is a character's **importance** – his or her position relative to others.

In some situations we look up to people because we see them as powerful, for example policemen, teachers and parents. But they could behave in ways which might make us change our view. For example, a police inspector who took bribes and told lies might lose his high status. A boy who had low status because he wasn't good at Maths and English could gain high status by being the school's top goal scorer.

Status is not always connected with obvious power or control, however. Two people who appear to have equal status can gain or lose it because of events. This could happen in the course of a scene in a drama, through something which is said or done.

Give each character in your drama a status number from 1 to 10, with 1 being lowest and 10 highest. Is each character's status the same all the way through? Can you improvise a scene in which status is changed by what happens?

In a drama about a teenage girl, her status might only be 2 when she is being told off by her mum about her untidy room, 6 when she's talking and having a laugh with her friends and 9 when she's asked out by the boy all the girls are keen on.

Learning more from being in an audience

You can learn a lot about building a character from watching actors in the theatre. Look at the programme to find out a bit about an actor's background. Sometimes there's a photo which can look quite different from the person on stage. Seeing the same actor playing different characters can show you how all the techniques you are learning to use can be put into practice. Notice how he or she moves and speaks. What gestures and mannerisms has he or she adopted? How is his or her relationship with other characters shown? Very often you see a character changing because of what is happening in the drama, making a kind of journey from ignorance to understanding. This can help with ideas for your own work.

CHAPTER 6
VOICE

In this chapter you will learn about:
- language and voice
- accent and dialect
- pace
- volume
- clarity
- emphasis
- pause
- pitch
- tone
- articulation
- fluency
- intonation
- register

Using your voice

Everyone is born with a voice of their own. We imitate the sounds around us as we grow up. This is how we learn our first language, and pick up regional accent and **dialect** words.

Your voice is produced by many parts of your body:
- vocal cords (folds of muscle and ligament)
- throat and mouth
- lips, teeth, and tongue.
- lungs, rib-cage and stomach muscles (all help produce breath)

In adolescence voices change. This happens at different rates for boys and girls. It takes time for your adult voice to develop. So it's best not force it too much as a teenager.

Your physical body is what you use in your work. You need to understand and care for it, including your voice.

Language and voice

Language is what we say, the words we choose and the order in which we say them. Voice is how we say it.

Accent and dialect

Accent is a way of speaking used in a local area or country – Dumfries or Dundee, Canada or the Czech Republic. You may want to play a role using a different accent. Recording the accent you want to learn and listening to it is a good way to pick it up. Allow the accent to drift into your own speech. Try talking back to the recorded voice, gradually feeling that you can carry on without the recording.

Some plays are written in **dialect**, and spoken in accent; not only are the **sounds** of the words different, but the words themselves.

Gregory Burke's *Gagarin Way* is written in West Fife dialect. In this dialect, there are some words which you probably wouldn't find in a standard dictionary, and the way the words sound is different to 'standard' English. For example, *ay* is pronounced like *eh*:

> Eddie is a factory worker, Tom is a security guard. The scene takes place in a storeroom which is part of a factory.

Eddie You ken we're no getting global warming ay?

Tom No.

Eddie It's gonnay be global apart fay us.

Tom Aye?

Eddie Something tay day way the Gulf Stream. The world heats up….. the polar cap recedes…..we stop getting the Gulf Stream…the world gets colder.

Tom You're joking.

Eddie Straight up. (*Beat*) A boy in the pub told me.

In *Mary Queen of Scots Got Her Head Chopped Off*, Liz Lochhead's character **La Corbie** sings a Scottish west-coast lullaby in a different Scots dialect:

> Wee chookie burdie
> Tol-alol-a-lol
> Laid an egg on the windae sole
> The windae sole it began to crack
> And wee chookie burdie roared and grat

Pace

Pace is the **speed** of speech. Often we speak quickly when we are anxious or excited. Words come more slowly when we are unsure of what to say. Notice your personal talking pace and that of people around you – friends, teachers, and family members. Try speaking the same phrase at different speeds and see how it affects the mood or meaning.

Someone breaking bad news might speak slowly, with hesitations between words:

> Please, sit down. (*Pause*) I'm afraid... it's not good news.

Someone with good news might find their words tumbling out at great speed:

> Mum! I-got-it-the-job-they-want-me-to-start-on-Monday-they're-going-to-pay-me-as-assistant manager-and-I'll-get-my-holidays-paid-as-well!

Volume

Volume is the **loudness** or **quietness** of voice. Speaking loudly enough for an audience to hear you requires more effort than normal conversation – actors must be able to **project** their voice so they can be heard clearly by the audience. At times, an actor may need to shout or scream. Unlike real life, where the scream or yell comes from something unexpected happening, in a drama, we can prepare ourselves and rehearse. Breathing in fully then breathing out with the sound will help you avoid straining your voice.

> Stand and deliver!

The highwayman's line, delivered with a gun in his hand, has to sound loud and commanding.

> **Cassius** (*aside to Brutus*)   You know not what you do: do not consent
> That Antony speak in his funeral

Cassius's lines are meant to be heard clearly by the audience but not by the other actors. This is where the **stage whisper** might be used – quiet but still clear.

Clarity

Clarity is **clearness** of the voice. Some physical habits that prevent us speaking clearly are hunching our shoulders, hesitating or mumbling. If we are afraid, the throat seems to close up. Free up your voice by singing or talking to yourself. Record your voice and listen to check how clear your speech is.

Emphasis

Emphasis is the **stress** on a word or phrase. Stressing certain words can change meaning. Here is a very simple example:

> I love you

> **I** love you
> meaning: *no-one else loves you, just* **me**

> I **love** you
> meaning: *I don't hate you, or just like you*

> I love **you**
> meaning: *I love only* **you**, *no-one else*

Pause

A **pause** is a **break** in **speaking**, or a **period of silence**. This can be very **effective** in producing realistic patterns of speech. A silence can be as effective as words in communicating feelings. Here is an example:

> I didn't want to tell you this (*Pause*) But I think you should know...

This pause adds tension and makes us wonder what comes next.

Pitch

Pitch measures how **high** or **low** the voice is. Children and women tend to have higher-pitched voices than men. A low voice may sound gruff and throaty, like Daddy Bear in *Goldilocks*; a high voice might sound shrill and squeaky (Baby Bear), while Mummy Bear's voice is somewhere in the middle.

Tone

Tone is a change of voice to **express emotion**. It lets us know how someone is feeling, for example angry, sad, hurt or pleased.

Try saying these phrases in different tones of voice and notice how the mood changes.

> I don't want to do that

> That would be good

Articulation

Articulation describes how **clearly** someone speaks – their **pronunciation** of words. There are lots of exercises to improve articulation – you probably know some *tongue twisters*. Here are a few to try and perfect:

Red lorry, yellow lorry

Sounding by sound is a sound method of sounding sounds

If you understand, say 'understand'.
If you don't understand, say 'don't understand'.
But if you understand and say 'don't understand'.
How do I understand that you understand? Understand!

A good stage presentation requires good **diction** – clear articulation and clarity of voice, so that words are understood clearly by the audience.

Fluency

Fluency is the way in which speech **flows**. Fluent speech is smooth and flowing. In this speech from *The Tempest* by William Shakespeare, the words help the actor to speak fluently:

Caliban   Be not afeard. The isle is full of noises,
Sounds and sweet airs that delight the ear and hurt not
Sometimes a thousand twanging instruments
Will hum about mine ears;

But realistic speech can be choppy and broken-up, not fluent at all. Here is an example from *Passing Places* by Stephen Greenhorn:

Binks *is phoning home.*
No...No ma...Fort William...Aye, Glen Coe was lovely...no, I'm not taking any pictures...
I'm not on holiday, ma, it's a business trip...
What?...Aye, alright I'll try and remember...
but look...I haven't got time to look for one wi a Highland Cow on it!

Intonation

Intonation is the **rising** and **falling** of speech – the **modulation** of the voice. For example, when you ask a question, your voice rises at the end:

Are you coming out tonight, then?

A very firm answer would probably fall, signalling the end of the conversation:

I told you already, no.

Chanting is a kind of intonation where everything is said on one or two notes. You might hear this at a football match:

Ea...sy, ea...sy!

Register

Register is a way of speaking **appropriate to a situation** or suitable for the person being spoken to.

The way you talk to your friends is different from the way you would speak to the head teacher at school. With friends you speak informally, often using slang words (see below). To someone like the head teacher you would be expected to speak respectfully – using the wrong register could get you into trouble!

Authority figures can give themselves status by using a formal register. For example, if you go to the bank to discuss opening an account, the person you approach might say,

Good morning, how can I help you today?

Sometimes we find an informal register is increasingly used in cafés and restaurants.

Hi, I'm Jason, your server for today. Our specials are on the board. Can I get you something to drink right now?

ACTIVITY

Teenage slang is constantly changing. Any examples I gave here would soon be out of date, so in this activity, you're going to make your own list of slang words!

Draw a chart like the one below with three columns. In the first column, write a slang word or phrase you and your friends use now. In the second, write down what it means. In the third column, write down a word or phrase people used to use for the same thing (ask your teacher or an older relative).

Word/phrase	Meaning	Previous word

Learning more from being in an audience

When you are watching a drama, notice first of all if you can hear what the actors are saying. Are their words clear? Are they using microphones or projecting their voices in order to be heard? What accents do you hear? Are they using a particular register? Is it appropriate? Be aware of how a change of tone, pitch or volume can change the mood of a scene. What ideas can you pick up for using yourself?

CHAPTER 7
MOVEMENT

In this chapter you will learn about:
- different styles of movement
- body language, facial expression and gesture
- eye contact
- posture
- use of space
- balance, speed and timing
- positioning and use of levels
- rhythm
- stance and use of direction
- mime, dance and mask work
- warming up.

Using your body

As with our voices, every individual **body** is unique. Becoming aware of our own natural physical potential and knowing how to make use of it is an important part of learning in drama. It is also essential to think about avoiding injury. Make sure your working space is clear and that the flooring is suitable for movement work.

Movement is a way of expressing ideas, emotions and relationships.

The two main types of movement are **naturalistic** and **stylised**.

Naturalistic movement

Naturalistic movement is realistic, the kind we use in our everyday lives. We use this to help build a character. We all have ways of standing, walking, using our hands and **facial expressions** which, like our voices, change as we grow up. Knowing your own **posture**, habits and behaviour allows you to take on other ways of using movement in your drama work.

Naturalistic movement involves:
- body language
- facial expressions
- gestures
- eye contact
- posture.

Body language provides messages to others given by the position or movement of the body. For example:

hands on hips, feet firmly planted

could mean

I am angry, I need you to pay attention to me

seated, with folded arms and legs crossed

could mean

Don't come close, I'm protecting myself

seated, legs wide apart, hands on thighs

could mean

I'm the strong one

Facial expression is a look which lets us know how someone feels.

Gesture is a movement of the hand or arm which communicates a message or emotion.

finger to the lips

could mean

keep quiet, don't make a sound!

index finder crooked towards you, beckoning

could mean

come here

raised fist, shaken

could mean

I want to hit you!

ACTIVITY

What do you mean?

With a partner, without using words, take turns to communicate only through gestures. How clear is the message?

Eye contact is how we look into someone else's eyes, for example:

- *looking into someone's eyes then quickly looking away and then back again* can be a way of flirting
- *gazing into one another's eyes* – two people falling in love
- *staring hard into someone's eyes* can be intimidating – who will look away first?
- *not looking into someone's eyes, deliberately avoiding eye contact*, can indicate contempt, fear, shyness or dishonesty

ACTIVITY

Look into my eyes

Working with a partner, try making different kinds of eye contact, from none at all to staring, and discuss the feelings which come up.

Posture is the position of the body, how it is held. Most of us will have a natural, comfortable way of standing. To learn to adopt a neutral posture as a starting point for all movement work is essential. Your feet are slightly apart and parallel. Your spine is aligned. Your shoulders are relaxed. Your head is balanced on your neck, centred and not tilted forward or back. You breathe easily and are relaxed.

You can then adopt a posture to suit your role in the drama, for example:

- *shoulders hunched, leaning forward, finger pointed* – the witch from Hansel and Gretel
- *on your toes, poised to strike, an imaginary dagger in your hand* – a pirate ready to fight the crew of a merchant ship
- *huddled on the ground, making yourself as small as possible* – the victim of a mugging.

Use of space is the way actors are positioned on the stage and in relation to one another. This can provide immediate clues for the audience. For example:

One actor striding downstage, head up, back straight, suggests confidence and purpose. The same person dragging their feet, moving into a corner, head down, shoulders slumped, looks tired and defeated.

Two actors walk onto an empty stage. What can we tell about their relationship by their use of space?

- *Close together, facing each other* – are they lovers, or about to start a fight?
- *At opposite sides of the stage, backs turned* – are they about to turn and fire pistols in a duel, or are they friends going their separate ways?

ACTIVITY

Hunter and hunted

In **pairs**, imagine that one character is trying to escape from another in a locked room and move around accordingly. Change over, discuss your experience of using the space, both as the pursuer and the pursued.

ACTIVITY

Friends and enemies

In a large group, each member decides on one person they want to get as close to as possible and another from whom they want to keep as far away from as possible. They have to do this in silence, without it being obvious. On a given signal, everyone moves around until given a signal to stop.

Discuss what happened. Did anyone work out who was chasing them or avoiding them?

Stylised movement expresses abstract ideas and uses movement in a creative way, through mime, dance drama and mask work. Stylised movement involves

- balance
- speed
- timing
- positioning
- use of levels
- use of space
- **rhythm**
- **stance**
- use of direction.

Balance involves keeping an even distribution of weight, on both feet, on tiptoes, on one leg, using a chair or raised platform.

Speed is how slowly or quickly you move, from running to keeping still. Slow motion is an effective way of drawing attention to a specific movement or **sequence**. Stillness can be effective – freezing a movement, or one figure in a group can highlight a key moment.

Timing is moving or pausing at exactly the right moment.

Positioning is where you are in relation to others and any staging – crouched in the centre of a circle or standing at the top of a set of **treads**.

ACTIVITY

Try out different positioning and **groupings** – individual, pairs, threes… Make contact in different ways – what shapes are emerging, what feelings are coming across?

Use of levels refers to low, medium and high body positions, for example:

lying, sitting, standing ⟶	low
crawling, walking, jumping ⟶	medium
Standing on tiptoe, arms stretched up ⟶	high

Use of space is similar to the use of space described in the **naturalistic** section above, but with the freedom to exaggerate positions and moves.

Rhythm is movement which follows a pattern or beat.

ACTIVITY

African Chant

Stand in two lines, A and B, facing each other. This chant welcomes the return of the sun, so the mood is very up-beat and energetic. A chants the line and makes the moves first, B repeats and copies.

A	*Ché ché kulé*	step right, stamp left foot, punch right fist then left
B	*Ché ché kulé*	repeat
A	*Ché ché kofisa*	step right, stamp left foot clap hands to ko-fi-sa
B	*Ché ché kofisa*	repeat
A	*Kofisa langa*	clap hands to ko-fi-sa, stamp right, stamp left foot
B	*Kofisa langa*	repeat
A	*Langa ché langa*	slap thighs lan-ga- ch-é- lan-ga
B	*Langa ché langa*	repeat
A	*Tum a dé dé*	side step, bend knees on tum and straighten on a dé dé
B	*Tum a dé dé*	repeat

Stance is the attitude or position of the body. Like body language, a person's stance can indicate status or mood. In stylised movement, stance may be exaggerated, for example:

...a triumphant warrior holds his sword high, his eyes gazing upwards, while his defeated enemy lies face down under his foot.

...the Victorian father stands erect, chin jutting forward, arms folded, while his weeping daughter kneels at his feet, her face upturned, her hands clasped, pleading for his forgiveness.

Use of direction refers to the ways we can move – up, down, forward and backwards, side to side.

ACTIVITY

Find your own path

In a large group, walk quickly in silence around the room in the same direction (clockwise). On a given signal (single drumbeat), change to the opposite direction (anti-clockwise). On subsequent drumbeats, change to any direction you choose, making your own path through the group, avoiding bumping into anyone.

Discuss how it felt to be moving with the group, then against the group.

Be imaginative in exploring the use of direction in a movement piece. Crossing the stage on a diagonal line (for example, walking from upstage right to downstage left) is a good way to let each member of a group be seen by the audience.

Movement can be **improvised** – allowing an immediate **response** to a stimulus (e.g. music or a drum-beat) or **rehearsed** – where ideas are developed and practiced.

Mime is a very specific form of **stylised movement** which can create an illusion of reality (e.g. being blown around by the wind, climbing stairs, handling imaginary objects).

Mime has to be:

simple   precise   exaggerated   clear   slow

In Shakespeare's play *Hamlet*, use is made of mime in the 'dumb show' which tells the story of the 'play within the play' This is sometimes done with the actors in masks (see page 57).

> A KING and QUEEN enter. They embrace each other lovingly. He lies down on a bank of flowers. She, seeing him asleep, leaves him. Another MAN comes in, takes off the KING's crown and kisses it. He pours poison in the sleeping KING's ear and exits. The QUEEN returns, finds the KING dead and mourns passionately. The POISONER enters and seems to share her sadness. The dead body is carried away. The POISONER woos the QUEEN with gifts; she is unwilling at first but in the end she accepts his love and they embrace.

In *Black Watch* by Gregory Burke, mime is used to show the emotions felt by soldiers as they read letters from home:

> The Sergeant enters with a bundle of airmail letters(blueys). Stewarty notices him and takes the letters. He opens one and starts reading it, the words giving him comfort. Another soldier enters and takes the remaining letters. Stewarty creates a sub-conscious sign language which expresses the content of his letter. One by one the soldiers enter, take the bundle of letter and, finding the one addressed to them, repeat the process for themselves.

The gestures used included hand on heart, hand to head, hand stretched out, and were repeated over and over again, with no attempt at being naturalistic, and therefore having a powerful emotional effect.

Dance drama

Dance drama is a way of presenting a drama using dance moves which might include running and freezing, a group moving in a circle, one figure being lifted by others, where the story is made clear through movement not words. Usually it would be set to music or sound of some kind. It could be improvised to express a feeling or emotion for the group at that moment or rehearsed for performance. You may have someone in your group who has dance training and may help suggest steps and sequences that could be used.

ACTIVITY

Using 'The Elements' as a stimulus, improvise movement to show each of the four elements:

EARTH   AIR   FIRE   WATER

Here are some ideas to start you off:

EARTH – everyone is at floor level, taking up hard, solid positions, bodies connected in threes and fours to represent stone and rock. Gradually slight movements like the shifting of the plates of the earth loosen and break up the groupings into individual boulders and pebbles, which roll and settle or move faster and become almost weightless, turning eventually to dust.

AIR – in a group, on tiptoe, a whisper of breath becomes a breeze, light movements become faster as the breeze becomes a wind, speed increases, the group breaks apart, direction changing as the wind becomes a gale, with whirling, wide movements taking up all of the space.

Now work out your own ideas for fire and water, keeping them abstract – concentrating on movements relating directly to the elements.

You might want to use music or sound effects to go with your dance drama.

Mask work

Mask work is where an actor wears a full or half-mask, so their own facial expression is hidden. The audience sees only the mask and the actor's body, so posture, gesture, movement, stance and positioning become the means of communication. With a blank or neutral mask (usually white or black), the absence of the face has a profound effect, transferring our attention to the rest of the body. You should be quite experienced in movement work and body awareness before beginning mask work, which is very challenging.

You can make a basic mask by using a paper bag big enough to go over the head without tearing. Make two eyeholes about the size of a 50p.

Masks which represent specific characters (such as Harlequin, The Doctor, and The Captain in a popular form of improvised theatre called *Commedia del Arte*) influence the actor's interpretation of the role. Masks which show different facial expressions provide very specific starting points for actors. Trestle Theatre, a major touring company produce educational packs for mask work of this type.

Here are a few simple rules for beginning mask work:

- keep the mask facing the audience
- make movements and gestures slow
- keep the hands away from the mask.

Learning more from being in an audience

When you see movement used in a drama, as all or part of a presentation, notice how it is done. Is it naturalistic or stylised? What use are actors making of body language, facial expression and gesture? How is the space being used? Look for changes of direction and levels. In a dance piece, notice repetitions of movement and changes of speed. How do the movements relate to the music?

ACTIVITY

Warm-up

Before you start a movement session or performance, you should prepare your body with a **warm-up**. Here is an easy warm-up routine you can do on your own or in a group. Make sure you have on suitable clothes (loose and comfortable) and footwear (trainers or soft shoes).

Start with a neutral stance (see Posture, page 53) and take several slow breaths, breathing in slowly, and out until all the breath has left your lungs. Check that your shoulders are soft and not lifted or tense.

Nod your head forwards and very slowly roll down, keeping your chin tucked under and your head close to the body, hands loose by your sides, swinging slightly forward as you go down. Bend your knees so there is no strain on your back and keep your shoulders soft. Keep breathing. Let yourself hang at the lowest point, head heavy, shoulders and arms loose. Breathe in and out again slowly. Now start to roll up, picturing the vertebrae (bony segments) of your spine stacking up, one on top of the other. Keep your head heavy and your arms and shoulders loose and free. Finally bring your head up to balance on your shoulders, checking that you are back in your neutral pose. You should feel grounded and centred, ready to move!

Begin to walk around the room, avoiding making eye contact or touching anyone else. **Focus** on your own neutral walk, making use of every metre of space on the floor. Now begin to notice others and adjust your walk so that sometimes you walk alongside someone, then turn and break away in a different direction. Make eye contact and notice how that feels. Speed up and change the pace to a fast walk, then a jog, taking care not to bump into anyone else, staying absolutely in control of your movements. Slow to a walk and then stop, finding a space of your own.

Now do some stretching. Reach up with your arms, keeping shoulders soft, reach out to the sides and then just stretch as your body feels like doing. Notice where you are stiff or tense, shake out your arms and legs. Gently bend and straighten your knees, going up on the balls of your feet to balance, then down and into a knee bend again. Remember to breathe! This can be a preparation for jumping or you can slowly let yourself relax, going into a sitting or lying position for a few moments and calmly breathe slowly, in through your nose, out through your mouth.

Don't force any movements – listen to your body and work at your own level, regardless of what people round about you are doing. Now you should feel energised and ready to begin improvising or rehearsing your movement piece.

CHAPTER 8
THEATRE ARTS

In this chapter you will learn about:
- design
- key roles
- lighting, sound and special effects
- props
- make-up and costume
- set and scenery.

Theatre arts

Theatre arts is the collective name for lighting , sound, costume, props, make-up and set. Any of these can be used to enhance a presentation.

Theatre arts will use technology and design. **Technology** is the hands-on equipment you need to get the effect you want, such as a CD player or **mixing desk** for sound effects or a dimmer board to operate lighting.

Design in the theatre means anything which the audience sees – the set (including scenery and furniture of all kinds), lighting, make-up, costumes and props. It can even include publicity materials like posters and programmes. The designer has to work closely with the director to make every aspect of the presentation look right.

Style and presentation

There are many different ways in which a particular play can be presented. Shakespeare's plays have been enjoyed by theatre audiences for 400 years and presented in many different ways. Often it's the design that gives a familiar drama a different slant. You don't have to have the actors in Elizabethan costumes – they can wear clothes from the 1920s or the present day. This can help make the play more interesting for a modern audience.

The style of the presentation will influence the design. A realistic drama may need a set which looks like a real place; for example, a hospital waiting room or a library. A box set, made from flats which form continuous walls, with opening doors and windows, could be used for this. Lighting would be used to give a believable indoor effect.

A presentation with a much freer approach to design might use a painted **backcloth** or a **gauze** (fabric which becomes see-through with a light behind it), moveable screens and rostra to create a number of different locations. Lighting would be used creatively to add colour, to **spotlight** areas of the stage and for special effects. These would provide mood and atmosphere for the drama.

While you are working on your own presentations, you will probably not have much time to think about design as a separate activity. But you may have enjoyed experimenting with make-up and costume, and using colour in creating a set and lighting effects. When you are planning a drama and working out how to present it to an audience, think about how you want it to look.

What you are able to use depends very much on the resources available in your school. You might have a fully equipped drama studio with a computerised lighting board, sound system and dressing rooms, or you could be working in a classroom with a CD player and a box of props.

You need to decide what effect you want and how you can achieve it. In the theatre, jobs responsibilities are shared out among a team. You can do this too, maybe with someone taking on several areas e.g. lighting and sound, costume and make-up. Here are some key roles:

Role	Responsible for:
director	interpreting the script
designer	overall design ideas
stage manager	all backstage activities and prompt copy
assistant stage manager	backstage activities and prompt copy (shares responsibility with stage manager)
stage crew	making scene changes
set designer	designing set and making a set model, scenery, furniture, providing ground plan for rehearsals
lighting designer/ operator	designing and operating lighting
sound designer/ operator	designing and operating sound
costume designer/ wardrobe manager	designing and managing costumes
make-up designer/ artist	responsible for designing, applying and organising make-up

Hint

What is important is that you know enough about theatre arts, design and technology to be able to say what you would use if you could.

The assistant stage manager might also be responsible for giving actors a **prompt** if they forget their place. The stage manager and assistant stage manager sit at the **prompt side** of the stage, which is usually the left-hand side of the stage.

You may also need someone to look after the **front of house** activities. These are all the things which relate to the audience, such as box office, refreshments, ushers and programme sellers.

Lighting

What lighting effects do you need? What kind of mood and atmosphere do you want? Would it help to light different areas of the stage for different scenes, rather than having to move scenery or furniture? You may not have the resources to do exactly what you want, but it is worth thinking about what you would do if you could.

You might have a **narrator** sitting **down stage** left who will need to be spotlit when she speaks, with perhaps two main acting areas lit when scenes are presented in two different locations. This would need careful positioning and **focussing** of suitable spotlights. The lighting operator would **crossfade**, bringing up one spotlight while fading down the other, with no **blackout** in between.

There are three main types of **lanterns: floods, Fresnel** and **profile spots**. Lanterns generally consist of a **lamp** (or bulb), and a reflector behind the lamp. Some lanterns have a lens in front of the lamp to focus the light into a beam.

Flood lanterns cannot be focussed and provide a broad **wash** of light

Flood lantern

Fresnel (*pronounced fre-nel*) spots can be focussed and provide a soft-edged beam of light. **Barn doors** can be attached to a **Fresnel**. These are adjusted to shape the beam and prevent the light spilling out of the lit area. You can always recognise Fresnel lanterns because of the circular ridges on the front lens.

Fresnel lantern with barn doors

Profile spots provide a hard-edged beam of light with a lens which can be focussed precisely. This type of lantern is often used for **follow spots**, which follow actors around the stage.

Profile spot

Gels are **colour filters** made of sheets of heat resistant dyed polyester film. The film is cut and fitted into frames attached to the front lanterns, changing the colour of the wash (flood) or beam (spotlight) of light.

Lanterns can be hung from a **lighting grid** or bar in the space above the stage, or mounted on bars offstage. They are held on with **g-clamps**, and a **safety chain** is used to make sure they cannot fall if the clamp fails. The lanterns are controlled by the lighting operator using a lighting desk.

Lighting desk used to control all the stage lighting

Lighting effects

For a realistic drama about a family you might need a daylight or indoor lighting state. For a science fiction adventure you might want to create an unearthly, creepy lighting state. These could be achieved by using different colours, for example straw and pink for the realistic presentation; green and blue for the fantasy drama.

There are lots of effects you can create with lighting. For example, you could use a painted gauze to make someone appear and disappear: lit from the front it looks solid, but with a light behind it you can see through it. **Gobos** in profile spots can be used to project a range of patterns like leaves or flames.

What equipment can you use? What are the safety rules? Can you change the position and focus of lanterns? Can you use different colour filters (gels)? What needs do other groups have? Often it is necessary to negotiate and compromise if groups are presenting their dramas one after the other. A few general lighting states which will work for all groups need to be agreed.

Who will operate the lights? This has to be someone who has some knowledge of your drama and has had the chance to see it in rehearsal. A clear list of cues (see **Script** section on pages 66–74 for more details) must be provided and time allowed for a technical rehearsal. This is to make sure everything works the way you want it when you want it.

The **lighting designer** should know the function of lighting, select effects and make and use a cue sheet.

Sound

What sound effects do you need? What music might you want to use before or during the presentation? Do you have percussion instruments like a tambour or tambourine, bells, chimes, or wood blocks that you can use?

You might use sound to create a mood – sad music from a film for an emotional farewell; owls hooting for a secret meeting in the woods at night. A sound effect could signal a key moment in the drama – a doorbell announcing the arrival of the police; an air raid siren in wartime interrupting a family meal.

Will these be live or pre-recorded? Sometimes it is easier to create a sound effect like a loud bang live off stage than to cue it perfectly on your sound system. You will need to find recorded sound effects or make your own. A suitable space and recording equipment will be needed as well as time to do this.

Your group will need to rehearse with the sound effects, to get the timing and volume levels right, well before the presentation.

Who will operate the sound equipment?

The person chosen to operate the sound equipment has to be someone who has some knowledge of your

drama and has had the chance to see it in rehearsal. As with lighting, a clear list of cues must be provided (see **Script** section for more details) and time allowed for a technical rehearsal.

The sound designer should know the function of sound, select music and/or sound effects, make and use a cue sheet.

> **Hint**
>
> You might see **LFX** and **SFX** on prompt copies of scripts – this is short for **Lighting Effects** and **Sound Effects**.

> **Hint**
>
> **Fading up** and **down** is the term used to describe lights being brightened or dimmed.
>
> **Fading in** and **out** is the term used to describe sound being made louder or quieter.
>
> Don't get them mixed up!

Costume

What costumes are needed to make characters believable? Is the drama set in a particular time in history? You might need to look at some books to find out what people wore in 1700 or 1914 (**period costume**). If it takes place in the future, you might use science fiction books, films or comics for ideas.

Think about simple ways of using costume to give the audience information about the characters. A white coat instantly suggests a doctor or a scientist, long skirts and shawls can help portray women from Victorian times, someone wearing a scruffy raincoat and an old scarf turns into a tramp. Wigs can provide a quick transformation.

> **Hint**
>
> Things that can be easily put on and taken off, preferably over school clothes, can save time and tempers.

Hats are very useful for quick changes of role, for example, policeman to builder. Personal props like briefcases and walking sticks can give the audience instant clues. Can some of your group provide their own costumes? For a drama which happens in the present day you can wear ordinary clothes which could be borrowed from home. You want to find something which suits the age and personality of the character. Could you adapt something to make it look right?

Make lists with information about what each person needs and where they are getting their costumes. Arrange time and space for trying on costumes; find somewhere to store them until the performance.

The costume designer has to select, make or adapt and organise costumes for each character, make and use a costume list.

Props

Think about which props you need. These could be personal props which people bring on, carry in pockets or wear – a gun, a hankie or spectacles. Set props, which are used in the presentation, have to be in place on stage at the right time – a phone, a plate of biscuits or a book. Props can also be used for set dressing, to make the drama more believable – comics and toys in a child's bedroom, a filing tray and a pot plant in the manager's office. Can you make some props – a letter or a paper fan?

What will you need to find or borrow – a stone, a skull? Avoid getting carried away with having too many props. They can make your drama more complicated for performers and take time to set up and put away. Using real food and liquids poses a special challenge and needs careful planning and management. Special props like (safe) breakable bottles and glasses are very effective but can be expensive.

Accurate lists are very important. You will need somewhere to store things safely. You will need a props table off stage where all props are kept when not being used. Don't let people put anything else on this! Make sure props are returned at the end of each rehearsal and performance.

The person responsible for props has to make a props list, select, organise and store props.

Make-up

Do you need to use make-up? Make-up is used to allow features to be seen under bright stage lights and to help create a believable character or effect. What you can do will be limited by what you are able to use, but it is useful to think about what you'd like to do, if you had the time and resources.

It may be important for someone to look old or ill. This doesn't need to be complicated. You could get away with something quite simple – a pale foundation base with some under-eye shading for the ill person, adding a bit more shading and some careful wrinkles to make them look old.

If you want to turn yourself into a threatening-looking criminal, you could darken your eyebrows, making them closer together, and give yourself some stubble using a stipple sponge.

A powerful female boss might wear a strong red lipstick – that might be all that's needed. In a small performance space where you're close to the audience, heavy make-up is not necessary.

Crepe hair can be used for creating realistic beards and moustaches. This is applied with spirit gum and takes time and practice. You usually need a special remover to take it off painlessly!

If you are presenting a futuristic drama, you may need very stylised, mask-like effects, using fantasy base colours like green or gold. Working out a design on paper first will make this easier to do quickly.

Perhaps a character is injured and has to be seen with a black eye or a wound. Bruises can be faked quite quickly with cream make-up in dark colours. Wounds and scars built up using soft putty or liquid latex will take longer. A tooth can be blacked out with a special tooth varnish. You might want to use a stage blood capsule in a fight scene for a realistic trickle of red from the corner of the mouth of the loser. This can be very effective but tricky to get right. It will need to be practised.

Do you have all the materials you need? Who else is using them? Where are you going to do the make-up? Work out designs, arrange to use suitable materials, do timed practice make-ups before your dress rehearsal. Some make-up companies produce make-up charts for specific types of characters. Allow time for applying and removing make-up. Hygiene is very important, with clean brushes and sponges used for each actor. Be very careful about possible sensitivity and allergies. It is also essential to leave all the equipment clean and tidy.

The **make-up designer** has to prepare make-up designs for each character, select, organise and use make-up.

Set and scenery

You will already have a ground plan which has been used and developed early in rehearsals. This is the starting point for your set. What do you need to create a believable set? If the drama happens in several different locations, how will you manage to show these?

Set model

What rostra and flats are available? Do you have a free-standing screen which could be covered with paper or cloth to suggest part of a room? Is there a moveable **rostrum** on wheels, called a **truck**, which could be used in several different ways: for example, as a street stall or a boat? Can you adapt or paint these? Can they be put into place quickly and easily? Can you avoid scene changes?

Think about making use of cloth to create an effect quickly and easily – a rectangular wooden rostrum with cloth draped over it could represent a table, a coffin or an altar. A free-standing screen could be draped with lengths of material to show a curtained window, the entrance to a cave…

Furniture

What furniture is needed? How will it be positioned? Take time to place furniture carefully, especially chairs. Make sure you are not going to mask anyone by having chairs too close together. Putting furniture at an angle to the audience can be useful.

Don't have more furniture than you need. You will need room to move around it easily. A hospital ward could be suggested with a folding bed with blanket and pillow. A school classroom could be represented by a few desks and some books. Small rostra and boxes can be used as stools and small tables. Mark positions of scenery and furniture with tape on the stage area to help with scene changes.

Special effects

For most of your drama work you're unlikely to be able to use much in the way of special effects, but it's useful to know what you could use if you had unlimited resources!

For a special presentation, you might be able to borrow or hire equipment. Even if you can't, you may be able to write about what you would have done.

A **smoke machine** can provide atmosphere – a foggy Victorian street, a dream sequence.

A **strobe light** can turn a straightforward movement piece into a flickering silent movie. (**Warning:** Strobe lights can trigger epileptic seizures, so you must always warn audiences if your performance uses strobe lights.)

Ultra-violet light creates other-wordly effects in a blackout, with white or fluorescent masks, puppets or costumes.

Pyrotechnics are stage fireworks which can help provide magical effects, such as a transformation scene in a pantomime. Explosives, gunfire and flares can give a dramatic backdrop to a battle scene. A licence is needed for anyone using this type of equipment.

Bubble machines, snow machines and splurge guns can be fun in children's shows and pantomimes.

Trapdoors can provide dramatic impact, for example a figure rises up from under the stage, or a body is lowered into a grave.

A revolving stage allows you to have two sets, which can be alternated for transformations and other effects.

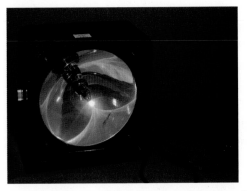

Strobe light, used for flashing lighting effects

Hint

Following safety rules is important for all technical work. Some effects such as flashing or strobe lights, require you to warn the audience beforehand.

Learning more from being in an audience

In the professional theatre, and in some amateur shows, you will have the chance to see Theatre Arts and technology used in different ways. Look at the effects and use your knowledge to work out how they are done. Shows like *Les Misérables, Joseph and the Amazing Technicolor Dreamcoat* and *The Lord of the Rings* use lots of special effects. If you are in a big theatre, look at the lighting rig – try to work out how effects are created. What colours are they using? Where are the lanterns positioned?

Sometimes you will see something quite unexpected – for example, the stage covered in deep earth for Northern Stage's *Animal Farm* or sand for The National Theatre of Scotland's *Realism* by Anthony Neilson or the collapsing house in *An Inspector Calls* (National Theatre).

CHAPTER 9
WORKING FROM A SCRIPT

In this chapter you will learn how to make use of a script, with advice on:
- directing
- blocking
- staging
- making a prompt copy

Using a script

Most of the work you do in drama is improvised, where you make up the words you say. But in the theatre, most plays you see are written by **playwrights** and the actors use a script to prepare their presentation. A script consists of the written words of a drama. It might be published, or your own original work.

The script is what the actors and the director have to work from. If you have read some plays aloud, you will know that it is quite hard to bring the characters to life in the way that you are used to doing in your own improvised dramas.

If you are keen to try something challenging, working from a script can be very rewarding. If you go on with drama beyond Standard Grade, you will be doing more work using scripts.

Here are some things to think about:

Some good points about using a script	Some challenging points about using a script
The storyline is worked out for you.	You have to stick to the storyline.
You don't have to think what to say.	You have to learn lines.
You get some ideas about moves.	You have to work out moves.

It takes quite a lot of time to take a script from page to stage, so it makes sense to work on a short piece to start with.

Here are some conventions associated with a script:
- A script is divided into acts and/or scenes
- A script includes a description of the set for each act/scene
- A script indicates changes of time and place for each act/scene
- A script allocates lines to characters
- A script includes stage directions

- A script includes advice to actors on delivery of lines
- A script includes ideas on how theatre arts can be used to enhance the drama

Not all of these will apply to every script.

Directing

Directing is the process of one person's interpretation of a script (or scenario) and development of it into a performance.

The director is responsible for:

- making the **meaning** of the script clear, helping actors make use of punctuation and other clues to understand the words
- **overall design** ideas (how theatre arts might be used)
- **communicating** and **liaising** with actors and design team
- **casting** (who will play which part)
- **blocking** (where and when characters move)
- the **rehearsal** process

How to work from page to stage

- Each person in the group should have a copy of the script which can be written on, in pencil. A pencil with a rubber on the end is a good idea – you can easily make changes with it.
- Give each person a part to read; it doesn't matter who reads which part just now. It's useful if one person can read the stage directions, so you can picture what's going on.
- Talk about what happens and what you think the characters are like. Work out where and when the drama is happening. Do some improvised drama, adopting roles from the script, to help understand it better.
- Now cast it; by now you should have an idea about who should play which part. It's a good idea if one of you can watch, listen and suggest ideas, taking on responsibility to direct. The director has to work out what the writer of the script is trying to put across to an audience. If you are directing, you need to have ideas about what the meaning and message is. Read it through again, with each of you now reading your own character's lines.
- Now you are ready to begin **blocking** your scene. Blocking means deciding where and when characters will move on stage and marking moves on the script. You need to think about what the audience will see. Avoid masking, where one actor is unintentionally preventing another from being seen by the audience. Note down gestures and any **business** – all actions on stage except gestures. Examples of business in the script on the following pages include brushing hair, playing the lute and putting the cord over the Princess's head.

Using stage directions

It helps when you're working on any drama (scripted or improvised) to be able to communicate quickly and easily with each other. Using words which are recognised in the theatre is a good idea. They seem confusing at first. This is because they go back to the old type of theatre where the stage was raked, sloping up from the audience so that the actors could be seen.

Here's a quick reference guide, with abbreviations and symbols (which save writing time):

Stage Direction	Abbreviation/ Symbol	Meaning
stage left	SL	actor's left
stage right	SR	actor's right
centre stage	CS	in the middle of the stage
up stage	US	area furthest from audience
down stage	DS	area nearest audience
move	→	go anywhere on stage
cross	X	move from one side of stage to the other
turn	↱	move round
enter	E	come in
exit	EX	go out
on stage	On	in the scene being played
off stage	Off	area close to the stage

Simple stage plan

USR Up Stage Right	USC Up Stage Centre	USL Up Stage Left
CSR Centre Stage Right	CS Centre Stage	CSL Centre Stage Left
DSR Down Stage Right	DSC Down Stage Centre	DSL Down Stage Left
Audience		

Decide on staging

When you decide on the staging of the play, you need to think about where your audience will be, and where your entrances and exits are.

You need to do a rough ground plan and to find some rehearsal furniture, just as you would for an improvised drama.

Get the group on their feet, with scripts and pencils in their hands. Now each person says their lines, but works out where they will stand, when they will move and what they will do. This needs good teamwork.

Listening to everyone's ideas is really important.

The director is responsible for making the scene work, to help bring the script to life, but it is still a group effort. Write down your moves as you go along.

The page opposite shows what a few lines from a script might look like. This one is adapted from a Victorian fairytale.

THE NECKLACE OF PRINCESS FIORIMONDE

The scene is the court room of the royal palace. The PRINCESS FIORIMONDE is seated on a couch upstage centre. Her three maids sit on the floor. YOLANDE plays a lute, EUNICE holds a box full of jewels, MELISANDE holds a golden brush.

YOLANDE   Which tune shall I play now, Princess?

MELISANDE   Let me brush your lovely hair, Princess.

EUNICE   Which jewels will you wear today, Princess?

Enter THE KING, stage right, walking slowly, deep in thought. YOLANDE, EUNICE and MELISANDE curtsey deeply. The PRINCESS goes to him and curtsies.

PRINCESS   Why are you sad, dear Father?

KING   My beautiful daughter, I am sad that I have no son to reign after me. We must find a suitable Prince for you to marry to be King after I am dead.

PRINCESS   There is plenty of time!

KING   No, you are old enough now. Ladies, tell my heralds to proclaim throughout the land that I seek a husband for my daughter. Those of high rank will be welcomed.

YOLANDE, EUNICE, MELISANDE *(together)*   Yes, your Majesty *(curtseying)*

KING exits left, followed by the three maids.

Alone, the PRINCESS frowns and stamps her feet. She raises her arms and moves them in a large circle, her lips moving. The room grows dark and there is a sound of thunder. The lights brighten and the WITCH appears beside the PRINCESS, carrying a black pot.

WITCH   Why do you call me, child?

PRINCESS   My father says I must marry but YOU know that I am not really beautiful, but ugly. I am not good, but wicked. You have cast a spell to make me appear beautiful and good, so that I would not tell my father of you and your wickedness. But if I marry, my husband will surely find out that you visit me. Then you will be killed and I will lose my beauty! What can I do?

WITCH   You must deal with each Prince as he comes to woo you. You must make them all into beads – the beads of a necklace such as woman never wore before!

PRINCESS   Yes, yes, a necklace!

WITCH   This is a dangerous spell – unless you are very careful, you may become a bead and hang upon the necklace with the others!

PRINCESS   I will take care – tell me what to do.

WITCH *(taking a golden cord from the pot and putting it over the head of the PRINCESS who now kneels before her)*
All you have to do is make each of your suitors close his fingers round the cord. At once they will be strung upon it as bright hard beads! But if you once join your fingers round the cord you will meet the same fate and hang upon the cord yourself!

(The room darkens to the sound of thunder and the WITCH vanishes.)

One script can be used as the **prompt copy**, on which all the moves are written down. This is the record of everything decided in rehearsals and is used to make sure everyone knows what they have to do in the performance.

Blocking is the slowest and often hardest bit. Be patient, stay calm. Now you can get down to serious rehearsing. Without the script in your hand you can really get into character. This is when you will feel the drama coming to life.

You might feel that you spend a lot of time hanging about, waiting to be involved, but you can learn a lot from watching. If you're waiting to go on or are already on stage without any lines, it's important to follow the script closely. Make sure you don't miss your cue (the word or signal for you to speak or move). Each move is

Script

(LFX1) (SFX1)

The scene is the court room of the royal palace. The PRINCESS FIORIMONDE is seated on a couch upstage centre. Her three maids sit on the floor. (1)

YOLANDE plays a lute, EUNICE holds a box full of jewels, MELISANDE holds a golden brush. (2)

YOLANDE (SFX2) (3)
Which tune shall I play now, Princess?
(4)

(5) (SFX3)

(6)
MELISANDE (7)
Let me brush your lovely hair, Princess.

EUNICE
Which jewels will you wear today, Princess? (8)

(9)

(10)   (11)

Enter THE KING, stage right, walking slowly deep in thought.

(SFX4)

(12)
  (13)
   (14)

YOLANDE, EUNICE and MELISANDE curtsey deeply. (15)
(LFX2)

The PRINCESS goes to him and curtsies. (16)

PRINCESS (17)
Why are you sad, dear Father?

KING
My beautiful daughter, I am sad that I have no son to reign after me. We must find a suitable Prince for you to marry to be King after I am dead.

given a number on the script, and the move numbers are written in pencil on the script to show when the move takes place. They are shown in red on the example here.

While rehearsals are going on, anyone in the group not needed for a scene can be getting on with technical work. As with any presentation, you will need to organise make-up, costumes, sound, lighting, scenery, furniture and props. Designs, lists, plans, lighting and sound plots need to be prepared.

Once you have decided where and when lighting and sound effects are needed, cues for these can be added to the prompt copy. It might look something like the example shown here.

Lighting	Sound	Moves
LFX 1 Bright indoor lighting	SFX 1 Tune played as if on lute	1 P is seated on couch USC. Y, E, M sit on floor immediately DSR of couch.
		2 Y mimes playing lute.
	SFX 2 Music stops	3 Y stops and looks up at P.
		4 P whispers to her.
	SFX 3 Music starts (tune 2)	5 Y smiles and begins to play again. 6 M moves upstage to stand behind couch, left of P with brush. 7 M brushes P's hair then comes back DS of couch and sits on floor in previous position.
		8 E holds up two tiaras to P. 9 P indicates one. 10 E puts down box, puts tiara on her head.
	SFX 4 Music stops	11 Enter K CSR walking slowly, deep in thought. Moves DSL
		12 Y puts down lute. 13 E puts down brush. 14 M puts down box.
LFX 2 Crossfade from indoor state to twilight state		15 Y,E,M move DSC and curtsey deeply to K.
		16 P moves DSL to stand R of K, half turned towards audience, and curtsies. 17 K takes P's left hand with his right hand and raises her to standing position.

Script

PRINCESS
There is plenty of time! (18)

KING (19)   (20)
No, you are old enough now. Ladies, tell my heralds to proclaim throughout the land that I seek a husband for my daughter. Those of high rank will be welcomed.

YOLANDE, EUNICE MELISANDE (*together*) Yes, your Majesty. (21)

KING exits left, followed by the three maids. (22)

Alone, the PRINCESS frowns and stamps her feet. (23)

She raises her arms and moves them in a large circle, her lips moving. (24)
(LFX3)
The room grows dark and there is a sound of thunder.
                    (LFX4)(SFX5)
(25) (LFX5)   (SFX6)
The lights brighten and the WITCH appears beside the PRINCESS, carrying a black pot.

WITCH
Why do you call me, child? (26)

PRINCESS
My father says I must marry but YOU know that I am not really beautiful, but ugly. I am not good, but wicked. You have cast a spell to make me appear beautiful and good, so that I would not tell my father of you and your wickedness. But if I marry, my husband will surely find out that you visit me. Then you will be killed and I will lose my beauty! What can I do?

WITCH
You must deal with each Prince as he comes to woo you. You must make them all into beads – the beads of a necklace such as woman never wore before!

PRINCESS
Yes, yes, a necklace!

WITCH
This is a dangerous spell – unless you are very careful, you may become a bead and hang upon the necklace with the others!

PRINCESS
I will take care – tell me what to do. (27)
(28)   (LFX6)   (SFX7)   (29)
WITCH (taking a golden cord from the pot and putting it over the head of the PRINCESS who now kneels before her)

WITCH
All you have to do is make each of your suitors close his fingers round the cord. At once they will be strung upon it as bright hard beads! But if you once join your fingers round the cord you will meet the same fate and hang upon the cord yourself! (LFX8)(SFX8)(30)

Lighting	Sound	Moves
		18 P turns away facing SR.
		19 K steps towards her, puts his hands on her shoulders and turns her to face him.
		20 K gestures to Y, E and M
		21 Y, E, M curtsey
		22 Exit KING CSL, followed by Y, E, M.
		23 P moves DSC, frowns and stamps her feet.
LFX 3 Fade to black LFX 4 Flashing lights, smoke	SFX 5 Thunder	24 P raises her arms and moves them in a large circle, her lips moving.
LFX 5 Spooky effect (greens and purples)	SFX 6 Spooky sound	25 Enter W DSR carrying a black pot. 26 P turns to face W
		27 P kneels and takes off tiara
LFX 6 Flickering effect (profile with rotating gobo) LFX 7 Fade up spotlight on Princess DSC	SFX 7 Magical bells (live)	28 W takes a golden cord from the pot 29 W puts cord over head of P
LFX 8 Snap to blackout	SFX 8 Thunder	30 Exit witch DSR during blackout

If you are going to present your drama to an audience, maybe to people outside your own class, you'll need to think about designing posters and programmes. Anyone with time to spare can do this.

You will need to spend some time with your group discussing progress. Everyone needs to know what is going on. Time needs to be allowed for actors to try on costumes and for sound and lighting cues to be worked out in rehearsals. (see Theatre Arts section for details of job responsibilities).

You can use all the skills of negotiating and working with others which you have learned in presenting your improvised dramas.

Learning more from being in an audience

If you are going to see a play, try to get hold of a copy of the script. The **National Theatre of Scotland** sells scripts for all its productions. Read it carefully, looking at the stage directions and any clues as to how the actors should say their lines. Imagine how you might direct it or stage it. Who would you cast for the main parts? Then compare the actual performance. How well did it work? Two productions of the same play can help you see how differently it can be staged. In class you may get the chance to work on script extracts, and to see other people's interpretations of the same material. This can teach you a lot about how to read and understand a play.

PREPARING FOR THE EXAM

Foundation, General and Credit

You will sit **two** of the three papers. You will either sit **Foundation** and **General**, or **General** and **Credit**.

The **Foundation** examination lasts **45 minutes**, and counts for **50 marks**.

The **General** examination lasts **45 minutes** and counts for **60 marks**.

The Credit examination lasts **60 minutes** and counts for **70 marks**.

Each paper is in two sections, **Section A** and **Section B.**

Section A is based on responses to the Stimulus Paper. Your teacher will give you the Stimulus Paper to study some time before the exam. Marks are allocated as follows:

Foundation	**25** marks
General	**30** marks
Credit	**20** marks

Section B is based on your knowledge and understanding of drama. Marks are allocated as follows:

Foundation	**25** marks
General	**30** marks
Credit	**50** marks

> **Important!**
>
> You will be expected to understand and use theatre terms (drama vocabulary) in both Sections of the paper

Working from the Stimulus Paper and preparing for Section A

Choosing your stimulus

Make a **good choice** of one stimulus from the options in the Stimulus Paper. Your teacher will give you help with this. When you get the Stimulus Paper some time before the exam, take time to read and study it carefully. The different stimuli in the Paper could be a poem, a drawing, an advertisement or any of the examples given on pages 10–14. Sometimes the stimulus that seems the most exciting to start with is the one you can't get very far with later on.

You need to be able to write well about this work in Section A of the exam, so make sure it has enough in it for you to use what you've learned. Remember that the stimulus is just the starting point. You can take your ideas in any direction as you create your drama. The more ideas you have, the better. You could try thinking of, say, two ideas for each stimulus, before you discuss the Stimulus Paper at all with your group.

Get the best from group work

All the skills you've been practising need to be used from the beginning. Reach a decision on which stimulus to use. As far as possible, allow everyone to choose how to develop their ideas. Maybe you could each write a scenario at home. Take the best suggestions and try them out through role-play. Use your knowledge of form and structure to agree on a scenario which is workable and has a message to communicate. Keep your use of theatre arts simple, but have more ambitious ideas in mind that you can write about.

Developing your characters fully, using all the techniques you've learned, is really important.

> ### Hint
>
> The examiner needs to know what you did in your group based on the Stimulus Paper.

Keeping notes

It's really important to keep careful notes from the start. Your notes are the basis of your answers to Section A. There is quite a long time between doing this practical work and sitting the exam. There is no way you can remember what you did unless you write or record it as you go along.

You must keep notes about:

- which stimulus you chose
- several reasons for your choice
- possible ways you could develop your chosen stimulus
- a scenario of your drama, showing which form(s) and conventions you are using, with a clear structure. Include time and place of each scene.
- details about your character – name, age, appearance, background, personality, interests, appearance, voice, movement, body language, gestures, motivation, relationships and status
- ground plans for each scene, with a key showing the correct symbols for furniture, set and rostra. Include positions of entrances and exits. Show where the audience would be.

- ideas about your target audience, purpose, the kind of venue you would choose and the reasons for your choice of form(s) and conventions
- details of theatre arts and technology, including ideas for: make-up, costume, sound, music, lighting, scenery, furniture and props

In Section A you must explain in detail how you **developed a stimulus** into a presentation.

You have to **outline a situation** suitable for acting out, showing that you know about **form** and **structure**.

You have to provide **detailed relevant information** about a **character**; and you must be aware of that **character's role** and **status** in the drama.

You must describe in detail how your drama could be **presented**, showing that you have thought about **target audience**, **staging** and **technical effects**. You have to give **reasons** for these decisions.

You should now have what you need to prepare for Section A of the Examination Paper. It's essential that you read the questions in Section A **very carefully** and do **exactly** what is asked. You must write in the **number** of the Stimulus chosen.

The questions in Section A may cover the points below. They may not be in the same order each year, and the precise wording may be different.

Here are some possibilities for points you will have to think about:

- different aspects of your own (or someone else's) character – voice or movement, status or anything else listed above
- relationships between characters
- the purpose of your drama and how well this was achieved
- who your target audience was
- a ground plan for the first or last scene of your drama, or for any scene
- a particular venue or way of staging
- an important moment or scene saying what happened and why it was important
- problems you had and how you solved them
- what theatre arts you would use and why.

If you have learned what is in your notes, you will be able to answer the questions in Section A.

Revising for Section B

The way to revise for Section B is to use your work from the course. Everything you've done may be relevant. However, you **must not** write about the work you did from the **Stimulus** paper in Section B.

You can use:
- your evaluations of yourself and others
- planning notes
- 'character cards' or other notes you have worked on
- writing in role
- homework
- recordings of discussions, work in progress, presentations of your own work and that of others
- notes made during class work
- answers to practice exam questions
- designs – set, lighting, costumes, make-up…
- reference books
- theatre programmes
- reviews of productions
- discussion with your teacher and others
- questions from past papers.

You could be asked about:
- the drama process
- voice
- movement
- **characterisation**
- staging
- forms and conventions
- tension
- mood and atmosphere
- drama terms
- purpose
- target audience
- relationships
- dealing with issues
- using research
- directing
- script work
- theatre arts and technology.

You could be asked about work covered in your course. For example, you could be asked how you developed a character or what you learned by being responsible for technical work for a presentation.

You might be asked to develop ideas for a drama either from a stimulus given in the question or for a particular target audience. To do well in these, you will have to write in some detail. Remember that you can use sketches and diagrams to explain your ideas.

There is likely to be a question which tests your knowledge of theatre words.

Always **look carefully** at what is being asked for. Read **all the questions** before you start writing. Notice **how many marks** are being given for each question.

Sitting the exam

If you've followed the advice about preparing for the exam you will be ready and able to do your best. You arrive in plenty of time.

You are told to start. You have 45 minutes for the Foundation paper, 45 minutes for the General paper and 60 minutes for the Credit paper. Remember, you will be sitting **two** of these.

In all papers, the first thing you see is the Stimulus Paper. That's nice and familiar. It's the same one you saw weeks ago!

Once you've filled in all your details on the front of the booklet, put your pen down and look through each section before you start writing.

Read the questions very carefully.

Notice exactly what is being asked for.

Are you asked for a Ground Plan for all or part of your drama?

What information is needed about character – your own or someone else's?

Use the marks as a guide to how much to write.

Don't spend ten minutes on a two-mark question; don't use lots of extra paper for a six-mark answer – it's not worth it. If you're stuck on a question, leave it and move on to the next. Try to make a point or justified comment for each mark.

Some questions may be divided into several sections. Read **all** of the sections before beginning your answer. Make sure you answer **all of them**.

> **Hint**
>
> **Read each question carefully and notice how many marks it's worth.**

Look at how much space you've been given for each answer. You don't have to fill it all up – people have different sized handwriting – but it does give you an idea of how long your answer should be. If you have very big writing, you'll probably need extra paper.

Don't panic! There's almost always a moment when you look up. You see everyone else writing quickly. Your mind has gone blank. Use your drama training – take a deep breath, relax your shoulders, close your eyes for a moment and remind yourself that this is drama. You are writing about what you know.

If you have a few minutes left at the end, look back through your answer booklet and fill in any gaps in your answers. Don't be tempted to change things at this point. Your first idea was probably right. Make sure your name and question number are on any extra sheets.

Time's up! You've finished your Standard Grade Drama Exam. And you've done your best.

How is your work in Knowledge and Understanding marked?

Your final grade will be based on the mark you are given for the written exam you sit at the end of your course. This is marked by an external examiner.

The exam tests all the Knowledge and Understanding you have gained during the course. If you've worked hard and taken the advice given to you by your teacher and in this book, you will have got the most out of doing Standard Grade Drama. That gives you a good basis for going on to study Drama at a more advanced level. All the knowledge and experience you have will help you, whatever course you choose.

Vocabulary list

This is a list of words used in drama. Some of these are words you may already know and use in other subjects such as English and Art, but the meanings given here are the ones used in Drama. Your teacher will tell you which words you **must** learn.

accent   a way of speaking used in a local area or country

acting   playing a part

action   events in a drama

actor   person playing a part

adopt   take on (e.g. a role)

apron   area of stage in front of the curtain

articulation   clear pronunciation of words

aside   a remark to the audience only

atmosphere   feeling created by environment; scenery, sound or lighting

audience   people watching a drama

auditorium   the area for the audience, generally filled with seats

avenue   audience seated on two sides of the acting arena

backcloth   canvas cloth which covers the back of the stage, can be painted

backstage   non-acting area behind the stage

balance   keeping an even distribution of weight

balcony   area of seating above the stalls and circles

barn doors   adjustable metal flaps attached to front of Fresnel spotlight for shaping the beam of light

blackout   the acting area is not lit
   slow fade: to black the lighting/sound is faded out slowly
   fast fade: to black the lighting/sound is faded out quickly
   snap: to black black out is achieved instantly

blacks   drapes which curtain off sides or back of stage, usually made of heavy black fabric

blocking   deciding where and when actors will move on stage

body language   messages given by the position or movement of the body

brainstorming   sharing and listing a large number of ideas

business   all actions on stage (e.g. opening a letter) except gestures

centre stage (CS)   centre area of the stage

centre stage left (CSL)   left-hand centre side of the acting area as the actor faces the audience

centre stage right (CSR)   right-hand centre side of the acting area as the actor faces the audience

character   specific person in a drama

characterisation   the process of fully developing a character

clarity   clearness of the voice

comedy   a drama which is funny/comical

communicate   tell, put across

conflict   struggle, fight, argument

content   what is in the drama, subject matter

contribute   offer suggestions, help to bring about

conventions   alternative ways of presenting parts of a drama (e.g. flashback, tableau)

costume   clothes worn by actors for their character

creating   the process of developing a drama's content and roles through practical exploration, experimentation and problem-solving

crossfade   to change from one lighting cue to another with no blackout in between, or to change from one sound cue to another with no silence in between

cue   signal for an actor to do or say something, or for a light or sound effect to begin or end

cyclorama   the back wall of stage which can be painted or lit

dance   artistic expression through movement

dance drama   a drama presented through dance moves

deadline   date or time by which a task must be finished

develop   make more detailed, build on, expand

dialect   way of speaking peculiar to a particular local area

dialogue   conversation involving two or more characters

diction   speaking clearly so that words can be understood by the audience

directing   organising, taking responsibility for interpreting a drama

docu-drama   a documentary style drama, including reconstructions of events

down stage (DS)   acting area closest to audience

down stage centre (DSC)   middle part of stage nearest the audience

down stage left (DSL)   part of stage nearest the audience on the left as the actor faces the audience

down stage right (DSR)   part of stage nearest the audience on the right as the actor faces the audience

drama   representation of life created through acting

dramatic irony   actions or remarks whose significance is not realised by all the characters

circle (dress, grand, upper)   areas of seating above stalls and below balcony

dress rehearsal a final rehearsal of a drama with all the theatre arts

effective having an effect, achieving what was wanted

emotion feeling

emphasis stress on a word or phrase

end on audience seated at one end, acting area at the other

enhance add to, improve

enter to come on stage

evaluate to judge the strengths and weaknesses of a drama

exit to leave the acting area

experiment try out

facial expression look on face which shows emotion

fade up/down brighten or dim lighting

fade in/out lower or raise volume of sound

filter coloured polyester sheet used for stage lighting (see gel)

flashback acting out an event in the past

flashforward acting out a future or imagined event

flat(s) wooden frame(s), joined together and covered with canvas, which can be painted
door flat: frame into which a door is built
window flat: frame into which a window is built

flies area above stage from where scenery/actors are flown in on pulleys

flood lantern giving a wide spread of light

floorcloth canvas floorcovering (sometimes painted)

fluency natural flowing speech

focus key moment, scene, character, relationship or event in a drama

focussing i) positioning a lantern to get the desired lighting effect ii) adjusting the lens of a spotlight to vary the size of the beam

focus on look closely at

follow spot powerful profile spotlight used to follow actors around the stage

form overall style of a drama

forum theatre the audience suggests changes to a drama in order to affect outcomes

freeze frame moment in a drama when action suddenly stops as if frozen in time

Fresnel spot lantern giving a soft-edged beam of light

front of house (FOH) any job in the theatre which involves dealing with the audience (e.g. box office, refreshments, usher)

frozen picture another word for tableau

gauze   see-through material which cannot be seen through when lit from the front but can be seen through when lit from behind

g-clamp   clamp used to secure lantern to lighting bar or stand

gel   film placed in front of a lantern, to change the colour of the beam

gobo   thin metal plate cut out in a pattern and placed in a lantern to pattern or shape into acting area

gesture   movement of hand or arm which communicates a meaning or emotion

green room   separate area where actors wait when not on stage

ground plan   bird's eye view of set showing what is on the set, entrances and exits and the position of the audience

group   more than two people

grouping   how actors are positioned, relative to each other

hot-seating   questioning a character in role

improvised drama   anything created and acted out by an individual or group

individual   one person

interaction   way in which characters behave towards one another

intonation   rising and falling (modulation) of voice in speech

issue   point in question, matter for discussion

justify   back up, prove with evidence

key   explanations of symbols used in a ground plan

key moment   one of the most important parts of a drama

LFX   short way to write lighting effect (also **LX**)

lamp   bulb for lantern

language   means of communication, through spoken or written words

lantern   stage light

lighting desk   control board for operating lanterns

lighting grid   bar used to suspend stage lanterns

location   place where the drama happens

make-up   worn by actors for their character

mannerism   habit of gesture or speech

masking   one actor unintentionally preventing another from being seen by audience

mask   a covering for all or part of face

meaning   what is meant to be understood

melodrama   sensational, exaggerated piece of drama

message   what is meant to be communicated

mime   stylised form of movement which creates an illusion of reality

mixing desk   control desk for sound effects being used in a drama

monologue   a character speaks their thoughts aloud

mood   state of mind or feeling

motivation   reason behind speech, movement or action

movement   use of the body as a means of communication

moves   actions performed by an actor

musical   drama which includes songs and/or music

narration   part or parts of the drama are told as a story

narrator   storyteller

off stage   area close to the stage, unseen by audience

on stage   in the scene being played

pace   speed of speech, movement or storyline

pair   two people

pantomime   Christmas theatrical entertainment usually based on a fairytale

pause   break in speaking, period of silence

performance   presentation of a drama to an audience

period costume   costume which reflects clothing from a particular time in history, e.g. Roman, Victorian

personal prop   an item carried or worn by a character e.g. glasses, handbag, wallet

physical   using the body

pitch   how high or low the voice is

play   another word for a drama

playwright   person who has written a play

plot   storyline of drama

portray   show

portrayal   how character is shown by an actor

positioning   placing of actors on stage

posture   position of the body – how it is held (e.g. upright)

present   show to audience

presenting   the results of the Creating process, including performance and evaluation

presentation   drama acted out in front of at least one person

profile spot   lantern giving a hard-edged beam of light

programme   information for audience which includes cast list

project   (of voice) throw, make audible to audience

promenade   audience follows action on foot, moving from one location to another

prompt   to supply forgotten lines to an actor

prompt copy   master copy of script with all moves and technical effects included

prompt side   left hand side of stage where prompter and stage manager sit during performance

prop (property)   object used by actor in drama

proscenium arch   stage within an enclosing arch

purpose   intention

pyrotechnics   stage fireworks

rake   slope of stage (to allow actors to be seen)

reaction   response to what happens

realistic   believable, like real life

register   appropriate speech for the person being spoken to, or for the situation

rehearsal   practice or preparation of a drama

rehearse   practise, prepare for presentation

rehearsed   drama devised/created without a script which is **improvisation**   rehearsed before presentation

reject   decide not to use, discard

relationship   how one person or idea connects with another, how characters interact

research   find out information

resources   anything which can be used

respond   reply, react

response   feeling, reaction

review   look back on what has been achieved

revolving stage   stage which turns in a circle

rhythm   movements which follow a pattern or beat

role   part played by an actor/attitude adopted

role-play   a means of exploring attitudes and beliefs

rostrum (rostra)   block(s) or platform(s) used to create a set at different levels

SFX   short way to write sound effect

safety chain   used to attach lantern to lighting bar for safety

scenario   outline of the plot of drama, including changes in time or place

scene   section of drama set in one place and at one time

scenery   resources used to create the setting where a drama takes place, e.g. backcloths, flats, rostra, furniture

script   the written words of a drama

select   choose

sequence   order of events

set (1)   scenery used to show where the drama takes place

set (2)   to place drama in a certain time or place

set props   objects on stage and used in the presentation

sight lines   what the audience sees of the stage from where they are sitting

situation   circumstances, specific point in drama

slow motion   movement performed at slowed down speed

soliloquy   single lengthy speech made when no other actors are on stage

sound effect   sound or music used in a drama
  live sound effect: operated on cue during performance e.g. doorbell
  pre-recorded sound effect: a sound effect is recorded in advance and played on cue

space   place in which drama is created or presented

special effects   used to create a mood or atmosphere e.g. strobe light, mirror ball, smoke machine

specific   definite

spontaneous improvisation   drama created 'on the spot' without a script or plan

spotlight   beam of light created by a lantern for a person or place on the acting area

stage directions   written or spoken advice on how to act a drama

stage manager   person responsible for all technical aspects of presentation

stage whisper   a loud whisper intended to be heard by audience

staging   the position of the acting area relative to the audience

stalls   lowest area of theatre seating, not above stage height

stance   attitude or position of the body

status   importance relative to others,

stereotype   exaggerated portrayal of a type of person

stimulus   anything which suggests ideas which can be developed into a drama

storyline   account of events, main facts of drama

strike (a set)   to remove all the set from the acting area

structure   the way in which time, place and action are sequenced

style   way of presenting drama

stylised   using rules of a particular style, often not realistic

tableau   a stage picture, held without movement

tabs   curtains

target audience   specific group of people at whom a drama is aimed

technology   equipment used to create effects such as lighting and sound

tension   build up of excitement

Theatre Arts   collective name for lighting, sound, costume, props, make up and set

theatre in the round   audience seated all around acting area

theme   subject, what a drama is about

thought-tracking   aid to characterisation: the character speaks their thoughts out loud

thought-tunnel   character walks past other characters who comment on their situation

thrust   audience seated on three sides of acting area

time   when a drama takes place (this could be time of day or historical period)

timing   speaking, moving or pausing at exactly the right moment

tone   a change of voice to express emotion

topic   subject for discussion or for drama

tragedy   a drama about unhappy events with a sad ending

tragic   sad, distressing

trapdoor   door in stage floor

treads   stairs

truck   piece of scenery on wheels for ease of movement

up stage centre (USC)   middle part of the stage furthest away from the audience

up stage left (USL)   left-hand part of the stage furthest away from audience as the actor faces the audience

up stage right (USR)   right-hand part of the stage furthest away from audience as the actor faces the audience

venue   place where a drama is presented

voice   sound uttered from the mouth, created in the larynx

voice-over   recorded speech played during a drama

voices in the head   recall of words said by others about a character or situation

volume   loudness or quietness of the voice

warm-up   exercise to prepare voice or body for acting

wash   effect providing even lighting over the acting area

wings   sides of a theatre stage

Ground plan key

Some pieces of stage furniture should only be represented using these symbols. Other pieces of stage furniture may be designed (such as the chest of drawers on page 22), but must be clearly explained in the key.

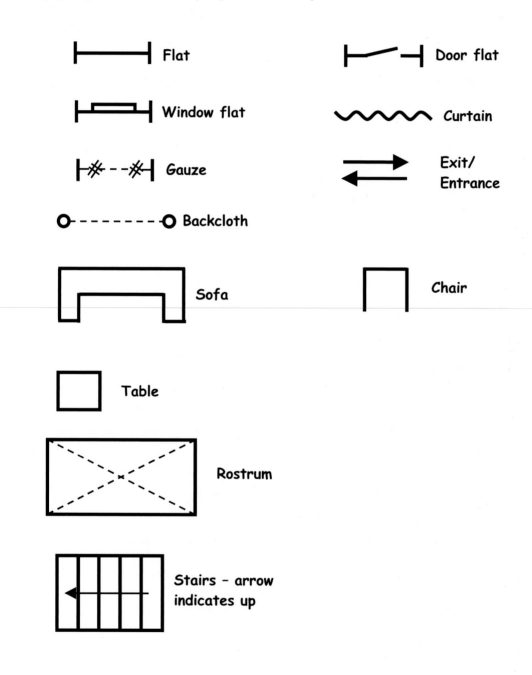